THE DIY PORN HANDBOOK

◆

A HOW-TO GUIDE TO DOCUMENTING OUR OWN SEXUAL REVOLUTION

◆

BY MADISON YOUNG

greenery press

Cover design: Johnny Ink, www.johnnyink.com.

Published in the United States by Greenery Press. Distributed by SCB Distributors, Gardena, CA.

MORE RAVES FOR THE DIY PORN HANDBOOK

"What is the future of pornography? *The DIY Porn Handbook* asks us to rethink porn for the masses as a grassroots art and political project, one that will redefine a culture of sexual commodification as the energetic expression of sexual liberation. Madison Young encourages us to roll up our sleeves and get busy in the work of making the kind of porn we want to see. Young's book empowers readers to create media, spaces, and conversations about sex that can revolutionize pornography and our society more broadly. Porn is political, didn't you know? – Mireille Miller-Young, co-editor, *The Feminist Porn Book*

"A smart porn primer with a fiery DIY punk heart. Madison's range is incredible; she details everything from story creation to camera angles to grassroots fundraising tips. It's a rare porn director who has both laboriously produced her own tiny low-budget avant-garde productions and helmed mainstream porn gigs as an experienced professional; we readers reap the benefits of what she's learned in both worlds." – Jennifer Lyon Bell, award-winning feminist porn director, Blue Artichoke Films

"*The DIY Porn Handbook: Documenting Our Sexual Revolution* is for anyone who has watched Madison Young's unique brand of erotic film and wondered how it's created from start to finish. In an age where the barrier of entry into adult entertainment is such that anyone with a smartphone can become a porn producer, Young's handbook comes just in the nick of time to help guide and inspire the next generation of do-it-yourself pornographers." – Siouxsie Q, *SF Weekly* columnist, podcaster, and author of *Truth, Justice, and the American Whore*

"The most useful and elegant how-to book ever written. Not only does it show us how to document our own sexual revolution, it offers the best history yet of that revolution and its far-reaching influence on our culture and body politic." - Constance Penley, co-editor, *The Feminist Porn Book*

AND APPLAUSE FOR MADISON YOUNG

"One of the most important feminist artists and pornographers working today... brave, brilliant, and one of a kind!" – Tristan Taormino

"Madison's love for the arts and her drive to support other artists makes her a special and unique symbol within both the sex industry and the art community. Madison has the ability to blend these worlds while maintaining both eroticism and intellect." – Dave Navarro, Jane's Addiction guitarist and author of *Trust No One*

"Making love is an art, and Madison Young is the Picasso of porn. She is the hottest, coolest, most movin' and shakin'est sex performer of today – and very likely of the next half century. Madison Young's performances are absolutely transcendental. She knows how to surrender to absolute ecstasy in just one breath. I've never seen a more erotically gifted pleasure artist. A truly enlightened slut! Madison Young is my porn art guru." – Annie Sprinkle, writer, porn star, performance artist, sex educator

"One of indie porn and the sex-positive community's brightest young stars. She puts her own body and eroticism on the line. And she documents her own sexual exploration and the interstices between sex and art so that even armchair erotic travelers can understand and vicariously experience these adventures." – Dr. Carol Queen, author, editor, sexologist

"Madison Young's pioneering work breaks boundaries. She is leading a new generation of 'post-porn modernists' as she deconstructs traditional concepts of the erotic and refigures them as artistic and educational performances that delight, entertain, and enlighten." – Charles Gatewood

TO A NEW GENERATION OF RADICAL DIY FILMMAKERS. BE BRAVE, BE FEARLESS AND ALWAYS FOLLOW YOUR HEART.

ACKNOWLEDGMENTS. I would like to extend my deepest gratitude to everyone who helped in making this book a reality. Immense love and gratitude to my fairy art mothers – Annie Sprinkle and Beth Stephens – for introducing me to Janet Hardy at Greenery Press and for being a continuous source of inspiration and love in my life. I'd like to thank my husband, my Daddy, my love – James Mogul. Thank you for your continual support in all of my many artistic endeavors. Your support and love mean the world to me. Thank you to all the amazing cast and crew that contributed their voices to this book and for creating DIY porn with me through out the years. Thank you to my friend, Cara Kelsey, for caring for my mini-feminista so that I could fit in enough hours to write this book. Much love and gratitude go out to my long time friend, Brian Kidwell, who introduced me to DIY culture within the music and literary world through punk bands, raves, and inky zines. To every volunteer, intern, assistant, and collaborator that has stayed after hours painting walls, hanging art, cleaning dildos, and flyering for events. Eternal gratitude to everyone who ever has or ever will give me a couch to crash on when I'm on tour screening my films, to everyone who comes out to the screenings, readings, and events. You are all essential to the DIY movement and I couldn't manifest these art-gasms, film-gasms, and word-gasms without all of you. To all those who have created radical art, film and porn before us and to everyone who will dare to pick up a camera and make their voice heard – my love, support and gratitude go out to you all for being a part of this movement.

CONTENTS

PREFACE: DIY PORN MANIFESTO

IN 1992, KATHLEEN HANNA OF BIKINI KILL WROTE "THE RIOT GRRRL MANIFESTO," which was published in the zine *Riot Grrrl*. Hanna's words, raw and full of youthful energy, fueled the new wave of feminist punk rock values, DIY ethos, and desire to create change in the world that they saw before them.

Her words were bold and unapologetic. Her manifesto was assertive and clear, it was a call to action and people listened. I listened.

Hanna's manifesto and the DIY riot grrrl movement and punk movement were a huge inspiration in my own development as a DIY artist and activist. In honor of Hanna's still powerful Riot Grrrl Manifesto, I chose to write my own manifesto as the preface for this book, a DIY Porn Manifesto, a call to action. I hope it serves as an inspiration as you go forward, as you discover your own unique voice as a DIY pornographer.

DIY PORN MANIFESTO

- Because we are tired of waiting for someone else to represent our bodies, our gender, our sexuality in a way that resonates with us.
- Because our voices matter. Our sexuality matters. Our gender expression matters and how we fuck matters!
- Because we refuse to live in fear of our bodies or quietly hide our pleasure and sexuality .
- Because documenting and archiving our sexual culture matters.
- Because no one else will do it for us and we refuse to be misrepresented, or have our stories exploited and commodified into the stereotypes that media wishes to shove down our throats.
- Because feminism and porn are important to one another.
- Because DIY porn is a powerful artistic medium and we refuse to back away from making it because of our gender or sexuality.
- Because art, film, porn, music is a *crucial* part of creating social change and radical activism.
- Because our world is deeply in need of a sexual revolution and we will smash the social stigmas surrounding sex, sex work, pornography, and any and all queer identities while advocating for healthy expression of self.
- Because sexual violence is real and we can change our society's relationship with sex through the creation of art, film and porn that advocates for consent, communication, safer sex and a healthy relationship to sexual desire.

1 DIY AND ITS INFLUENCE ON PORN

I STAND ON ONE HIGH-HEELED FOOT, WEARING NOTHING BUT a black lace garter belt and stockings. My other leg is bound in a tree-like yoga position, and my arms are tied behind my back with crimson hemp rope. My rouged mouth is stuffed with a blue ball gag, and a lampshade rests on top of my head.

"Ut!" I project from under the lampshade.

"I think she said 'cut'," my videographer says to the crew as my co-star – Jewell Merceau – removes the lampshade from my head, and the gag, gently, from my drooling mouth. Jewell squirts some water from my nearby water bottle into my open lips.

"Thank you," I say, looking up at her. "Um, so how did that look? Did you get a close up of the vibrator on my pussy? I'd really love if we can get a shot with the camera on the floor, gazing up into the lampshade as I'm orgasming. With luck, we can even get some drool dripping downward toward the lens."

My leg is shaking in its high-heeled shoe. My hands are going purple, my arms are still bound, the tips of my fingers are starting to tingle. My videographer shouts, "You got it, boss," and my co-star places the drooly blue ball gag back in my mouth. I close my eyes, inhale, exhale and project in a muffled voice from behind my gag, "Action."

◆

That was my directorial debut, but certainly not the last time I would direct with a ball gag in my mouth or wrapped in tight bondage. Bondage, I knew. Pain, I understood. But when it came to directing, I didn't know what I was doing.

I had never directed a film before, but I knew I wanted to make films. I knew I didn't want to just participate as a performer in someone else's stories, I wanted to create space for my own fantasies to come alive in front of the camera.

At the time – in 2005 – I had never heard the term feminist porn. I hadn't heard the term DIY porn. However, I was a very active part of the feminist art and DIY art movements, and I wanted to see what would happen if I applied my feminist and DIY community organizing skills to porn. What if I created porn from my own fantasies? What if I told stories about sexuality through my own lens (which happened to be a feminist kinky queer lens because I was a kinky queer feminist)?

I was not a trained filmmaker. In fact I wasn't a trained gallerist or curator or artist. I simply *was* all those things because they made sense to me; these were things I did. I was passionate about them, and I didn't let anything stand in the way of my making art, curating exhibitions or making porn. I knew the importance of mentorship – of surrounding myself with artists, filmmakers and pornographers who inspired me. I watched how they worked, and then figured out the rest by doing it.

I had an advantage when I started directing, as I had been performing and modeling for several years already. I'd worked constantly, averaging around a dozen shoots per month. A porn set was like a second home, and I knew the inner workings of a film shoot from a performer's point of view.

By 2005, when I directed and produced my first feature film, *Bondage Boob Tube*, I had modeled for or performed in around three hundred photo or video scenes. I knew my way around a production set, knew how to be resourceful, and was aware, as a performer, of the key elements to bringing out my best performance. I also had the advantage of having already met videographers, crew and performers who were aligned with my ethos, based on productions in which I had performed. With these skills and resources, I set out to write my first script, knowing that I'd make mistakes along the way.

A decade later, I have directed forty-two feature-length erotic films. I've made my fair share of mistakes, and reveled in some glorious successes in DIY porn making, including numerous nominations and awards for my filmmaking and screenings at film festivals around the world.

The DIY Porn Handbook is not a book that will prevent you from failing. It is a book that encourages you to fail, and to fail often. I have had failures and successes with all forty-two of my feature films and I am still learning and growing with every production. This is a book that I hope will encourage you to follow your passion, to write the stories that burn brightly in your heart and keep you awake at night, to manifest your dreams and work through your fears. I want you to create films – not that you think will sell really well – but films that you dream about, that inspire you, that make you blush, that make your heart warm, that you want to see on a big screen. I'm talking about films whose performers and communities can stand beside you with pride in your collaborative process, as they declare that they were a part of something you created.

Create something that you are proud of. Create a revolution, a change, something true and full of beauty. I hope that this book gives you the tools and inspiration to create not just another porn flick in the world, but a film that invites the world into a unique view of sexuality, connection and pleasure. I hope that this book encourages you to create art, and to articulate and explore your fantasies, both in front of the camera and as part of your own personal sexual revolution.

MAKE YOUR OWN PORN OR DIY TRYING

DIY doesn't mean kitsch or crafts or a commodification of cool. As I use the term DIY in this book, it means that no one is going to do it for us, so we have to do it for ourselves.

I first heard the term DIY in the context of music. As someone who was immersed in music and art subcultures that veered from the mainstream, I understood quickly that no one was going to bring our favorite punk bands to our venues. No one was going to organize the punk shows we wanted to attend. No one was going to invite loud, feminist, spoken-word artists into their traditional venues. No one was going to create the books and magazines, record our bands, or fuel the changes that we were so hungry for. So if we didn't Do It Ourselves, our voices would go unheard and we would remain in a place of disempowerment – waiting for others to validate our lives, our music, our sex, our political interests and our voices.

DIY emerged from this knowledge, and a fearlessness. We weren't afraid to fail. Failure was sitting by and waiting for someone else to make something happen. What resulted from this movement was punk, emo, screamo, hardcore, queercore bands playing at house parties, music stores, coffee houses, VFW halls and Mr Tuxedo shops after hours.

DIY birthed radical feminist zines. I remember the fresh and inky smell of warm xeroxed chapbooks that we copied after hours at Kinkos, because our friend's friend Christine worked there and could get us free copies. DIY made room for loud booming raves in cornfields, nights of music that seemed to never end, and underground locations that you'd spend half the night searching for. Our DIY generation was determined to create space for self-expression by any means necessary, and we did.

It was this DIY spirit that ignited my own desire in founding the DIY Femina Potens Art Gallery in 2000. I was twenty years old. I hadn't finished college and I was having a hard time convincing myself that I needed to go further into debt in order to live out my dream as an artist in San Francisco.

When I moved to San Francisco, there were very few all-ages venues. The city was just coming out of its first dot-com boom that had wrought havoc on the Bay Area arts community. I bounced from couch to couch, sometimes spending the evening drinking bottomless cups of coffee at twenty-four-hour diners, and wandering the streets when I couldn't find a couch to crash on.

While I was still couch-surfing, I rented a one-car garage in the upper Haight, under the name Femina Potens Art Gallery. This was the birth spot of our first few DIY art shows. Eventually, I found a secure apartment and got a small loan that let me sign a lease on Femina Potens' first real storefront location.

As my DIY arts organization continued to expand, and we built up our programming, I had the pleasure of meeting many of my artistic and literary heroes, such as Carol Queen, Michelle Tea and Annie Sprinkle.

To support and supplement my arts organization and my own artistic endeavors, I started my journey into sex work, and was inspired by strong feminist sex workers who spoke and created art about their experiences in the sex industry. These women were able to navigate the complicated power exchanges inherent in sex work.

I recognized within the feminist and sex worker communities a DIY ethos, again coming from necessity. We were women, queers and sex workers. People weren't going to make things happen for us; we had to do it ourselves, or again our voices would not be heard. DIY was a creed, a promise, a vow we made to one another – that we were committed to making something work outside of the prescribed processes that had been previously dictated. We were resourceful, working with what we had. More often than not this meant operating with limited financial resources. DIY meant we were scrappy and self-determined, following our hearts and our passions.

In 2002, I started working at the unionized peep show, The Lusty Lady. During this first venture into sex work I was reading the work of Carol Queen – *Real Live Nude Girl*, and Annie Sprinkle's *Post Porn Modernist.* I quickly started modeling for local fetish photographers and dipping my toes into pornography as a way to support my life as an independent artist. I saw it as simply another extension of my art; it gave me something to make art about – a study of human sexuality and desire – a study of my own sexuality and desire.

As I continued my study of the pornographic climate of the new millennium, I found a familiar ache rising inside me. I ached with a desire to explore sexuality beyond the prescribed script of pornography that was being repeated time and time again. It was this same ache that had motivated me to curate DIY art shows, throw DIY punk shows, make zines about female ejaculation, and create DIY chapbooks like *The Cycle* that focused on women's reproduction. That's what I was feeling: that same ache.

All smiles after winning Best Lesbian Vignettes at the 2014 Feminist Porn Awards for my docu-porn *Women Reclaiming Sex on Film.*

If pornography was an art form – which I believe it can be – and the DIY movement depended on the voices of outsiders, utilizing their words, images and music to create social change, couldn't the DIY art movement and pornography intersect?

I picked up a camera and started reading books on filmmaking. I immersed myself in erotic imagery and lush, compelling films that inspired me, and started deconstructing them.

On a Greyhound bus, on a coffee-stained napkin, I started to storyboard my first film. I was headed from LA to Seattle for a DIY touring art show I had curated – The Traveling Erotic Art Show – featuring some of my favorite erotic photographers, like Steve Diet Goedde, Dave Naz, Chas Ray Krider, Julie Simone, Lochai and Barbara Nitke. The film I had started to storyboard would become the 2006 Feminist Porn Award winning film, *Bondage Boob Tube.*

2 THE HISTORY, PRESENT AND FUTURE OF DIY PORN

BEFORE WE DELVE INTO HOW TO MAKE DIY PORN, let's define what porn is and what it can be. DIY porn, as I define it, is a product of communities and groups documenting their own sexual culture.

DIY porn is simultaneously a socio-political movement and an artistic movement and mode of expression. It lends itself to the empowerment of communities and cultures to tell their stories, and to embrace and celebrate their sexual identities, relationships, desires, connections, fantasies and beyond. The scope of this genre of film is as huge as the social stigma that comes attached to it.

The word "porn" gets a bad rap. It's loaded, and rife with stigma. Porn is a four-letter word, written in scarlet-red letters. Porn is a word that, when uttered, can spark fear, anger, inadequacy, jealousy, hurt, shame and disgust in a roomful of people. PORN. It's powerful. It's an emotional word. It's packed. It's heavy.

Many people have negative feelings around the word. Porn has been a container to hold our repressed sexual fantasies, a container and a closet that absorbs all the shame our society feels around its sexual desires. Porn becomes the scapegoat for sexual shame.

We are told that porn is shameful – whatever makes us uncomfortable in our sexuality is not our fault, but the fault of porn – that we are damaged in our view of sexual connection and healthy sexual expression. Porn is portrayed as a dirty, subhuman level of commercialism that takes advantage of its viewers' weaknesses by luring them in with erotic imagery. We're led to believe that those who perform in porn are desperate, exploited victims who lack the ability to choose what they do with their bodies. We are sold the idea that sex isn't something that should be public, that it is a private act, and that anyone who chooses to perform a sexual act in front of a camera must be damaged.

In reality, all porn is not the same, just as all sex is not the same. The ways in which people share affection and intimacy vary greatly.

Porn is a genre of film, just as comedy, thriller, adventure, drama and documentary are genres of film. Pornography is becoming more and more diverse in its exploration and documentation of sexual desire, thanks to a growing DIY and feminist porn movement, greater access to production equipment and technology, and ever-expanding vehicles of distribution.

The focus of this book is DIY porn – which assumes that you will be hands-on in the process of making and producing the film(s) that you aspire to create. Know that one of the empowering elements of DIY is that there are no hard and fast rules, no one way to produce and create a film. I encourage you to experiment with different techniques and guidelines provided in this handbook; see what works for you, modify, and feel inspired to operate totally outside of the box.

Porn has been a crucial part of our history, just as sex is a crucial part of our history, our culture and the relationships that we build. Porn is therefore a powerful medium in which to work, as it represents a documentation of sex, sexuality and eroticism.

It is a medium that creates space for viewers to connect with their own desires.

Working in the realm of porn for well over a decade now, I've discovered how truly transgressive it is to be articulate about your sexual desire, to communicate about pleasure, and to document authentic sexual connection in a way that expresses to the viewer, it's okay to like sex. Really, it's okay.

I am troubled by the degree of hatred and fear knotted up in the pit of our society's gut around sex. But when someone creates a safe space to discuss sexuality, desire and porn, I've found that most people are eager to be a part of the conversation. Many want to help chip away at the enormous stigma that infringes on healthy, open communication about our desires and fantasies in our sexual relationships.

As someone who creates DIY porn and speaks publicly on the topic, I hear from the public about how porn has impacted their sex lives, their relationships with partners, their relationships with their own bodies, and their own desires. Porn is a powerful artistic medium. It is a medium in which artists can work and absolutely transform how someone might feel about desire, exploration, kink, fetish, sex work, feminism, sexual identity and more.

Few people that you speak with will have had a seamless relationship with the medium of porn. It is often something that they hid as teenagers – magazines stashed under mattresses, or browser histories deleted. And if you are found out, if your porn is discovered and the images that turn you on unveiled, then your unspoken desires are known by another. You could die of shame, of embarrassment. What a pervert you are for gazing at porn, for responding to a film or image in which someone is acting out their sexual fantasies! How deviant!

Or is it, really?

Our sexuality is closeted from the public, while simultaneously throbbing to escape its confines in overtly sexual advertisements, billboards and pop culture. Sitting down with our partner to talk about our sexual desires is terrifying and therefore all too rare.

Our society shames our bodies and sexual desires, then capitalizes on the "hush-hush" behind-closed-doors eroticizing of the fantasies that are spoon fed to us. These are the fantasies we are told we should consume... but quietly. Sex workers, whores and porn stars are loud and brash about their sexual desires; they are damaged victims (or so we are led to believe). The rest of you must keep your erotic desires quieted and quelled behind the curtain. Shhhhhhhhhhhh!

Well, fuck that! DIY porn is the art of documenting and creating radical films about our own desires and fantasies. DIY porn boldly and bravely encompasses our own narratives, and our own viewpoint of the world and of sexuality. This is the way that we like to fuck, these are the people that we like to fuck, and we are making the choice to fuck.

We are taking control of the narrative, the camera and the lens. We are not compromising our fantasies or desires to meet any given audience's expectations of what, who or how we should be expressing our own sexual desire. That is for us to choose. We are telling our own stories and embracing who we are – our identities, our gender expression, our culture, our bodies, our sexuality, our relationships, and all the fragments that pull together to make us who we are and inform our sexual selves.

DIY porn doesn't hide the parts of ourselves that make us who we are, that make us individuals; instead it celebrates them. We love ourselves – not despite the parts of us that don't neatly fit into the mainstream boxes with which we've been presented, but because of them.

When we live boldly and without fear in our own skin and our own bodies, in front of the camera, riding waves of unleashed sexual pleasure and howling out in unapologetic orgasm for all to see, we are empowering not only ourselves, but everyone who bears witness to that act in viewing our films. We are changing our culture and the way that we perceive and talk about sex and porn.

I don't think that pornography's sole purpose should be to educate our society, but I do know that it provides an opportunity to advocate for healthier sexual communication through graphic modeling of sexual negotiation and expression of our sexual desires. If we can shift the imagery and portrayal of sexual expression, exploration and communication, then we can create space to lead our culture into a healthier form of sexual expression and an overall healthy view – of our bodies, of pleasure and of relationships with ourselves and others.

Each DIY porn film has the ability to smash sexual stigma and give us a new language to discuss desire, along with the space and permission to do so.

So do so.

Welcome to DIY porn.

As DIY pornographers, we are gifted with a great freedom. We are not under the financial constraints of production studios that require us to simply generate content that will feed the masses what they have been trained to consume – pornography that fuels sexual inadequacy, feeds our insecurities and perpetuates sexual shame.

As DIY pornographers we can create low-budget films that question this relationship with sexual material and our own sexuality, and advocate for a different view of sexual expression, one that advocates for pleasure, connection and communication.

So where will DIY porn lead us? What is the new future of pornography? What I see happening in porn is people who are ready for change. I see people who are looking for something new, who are becoming more aware of their sexuality, their desires and their needs, and they are speaking up. They are taking action.

There is so little standing in the way of us having our voices heard, to documenting our own sexual revolution. How exciting is that? Right now we have greater access to watching, viewing and distributing our films on our own terms, in our own way, to our own communities, than ever before.

A rising number of women are picking up the camera; folks of gender variance, the trans community, differently abled folks, people of all body sizes, orientations, gender identities, ethnicities, from a wide array of cultures, they are all making the porn they have always wanted to see. They are documenting their fantasies! This is a brave and revolutionary act, and I encourage you to do the same. I hope that this book aids you in your process of DIY porn making as you expand the definition of what DIY porn is and what it can be.

Presenting an award for Best Emerging Filmmaker at the 2010 Feminist Porn Awards in Toronto.

3 WHY DOES DIY PORN MATTER?

NOW YOU HAVE STARTED TO FORM A CLEAR IDEA OF what DIY porn is, but why does it matter? What is the importance of documenting authentic sexual pleasure?

Documenting authentic sexual pleasure grants permission and creates space for viewers to recognize, explore and express their own authentic sexual desires. It also works to de-stigmatize sexuality and serves as a chance for us to view sex and sexual desire outside of a shamed mode of expression.

When you think about it, pornography is the only cinematic medium – and one of the only modes of artistic expression – that dares to document, capture, examine and reflect upon our sexual culture. It is the only visual medium we have that captures graphic sexual intimacy and sexual relationships. In this way, pornography is a truly powerful medium of artistic practice. By creating pornography that reflects healthy sexual communication, pornography can provide graphic modeling for healthier sexual communication.

If the pornography we are shooting honors each performer as an individual, and models individuals stating their sexual needs and desires, with preferences like, "Baby, I really love it when you suck on my nipples, but I think it would be so fucking hot if you slap me on the face instead of licking my cunt. That would get me so turned on. I'll show you how I like it." Or, "How does it feel when I rock on your g-spot with my fingers like this? Does that feel good? You feel so wet. I love it." "Mmm, yes, that feels really good, and baby I'm so wet for you. It would feel even better if you slip on some of the latex gloves and squirt some more lube on my cunt. That would feel so good." "Like this?" Snap of glove. "Oooh, I love that sound. Yes, that's perfect, my love."

This type of dialogue within a film models communication, desire, feedback without judgment, connection, safer sex practices and negotiation (as well as the use of lubricant, and a way of asking for lubricant that feels sexy and not awkward). When people see clear communication and safer sex practices being used, and authentic pleasure being expressed in a way that is natural and not exclusively focused on the orgasm, but on pleasure and partnered intimacy and connection, it radically shifts their perception of sex, and models for them a way to ask for what they want in the bedroom.

Documenting authentic sexual pleasure allows us the freedom to be ourselves. We see and recognize a diverse representation of desires and fantasies that are lived out, communicated, and birthed in a wide variety of expressions. It also expands the way we perceive beauty, who engenders desire, and who is desirable. DIY porn expands our minds to include images, sexual stories and narratives of a wide variety of body types, gender expressions, ethnic and cultural backgrounds, and differently abled bodies. Some of my first encounters with this expanded vision of beauty and the sexual celebration of diversity in erotic film were rooted in the "alt porn" movement, spearheaded by companies like Joanna Angel's Burning Angel, Eon McKai's Vivid Alt Films, and the soft core pin-up imagery of the Suicide Girls and Super Cult websites.

These DIY indie porn pioneers were part of the punk, hard core, art core, body modification and indie music culture. When they didn't see themselves and their cultures represented in erotic film and narratives, they responded by starting to create films and imagery that represented their own communities. Many of the alt community's models were heavily tattooed, had numerous body piercings, and their hair might be shaved, spiked into a mohawk, or colored any color of the rainbow – a dramatic variance from what was represented in mainstream pornography. They were bold and authentic in their outward expression and celebration of self, both with and without clothing.

I recall one popular model on Suicide Girls – Amina Suicide – stating in a blog post that ran with the release of one of her photo shoots that she had a prosthetic leg. In some of her earlier photo shoots she'd cropped her photos to avoid revealing her disability, but then decided to come out on the SG forum. Her prosthetic was custom-tattooed to match the beautiful art that adorned the rest of her body. She was beautiful and brave and was met with loving kindness in the SG community as she shared her story and revealed and celebrated her body and sexuality openly. Amina was celebrated as the beautiful individual that she is, not as someone who was fetishized for her difference – which is often something we find within mainstream pornography.

In 2003, I curled up with my then-girlfriend Gauge on the couch in our Castro apartment, eyes glued to the television screen. We were giddy with anticipation to watch queer porn pioneers SIR Video's *Sugar High Glitter City* (released in 2001). The film was produced and directed by the powerhouse duo Shar Rednour and Jackie Strano, who portrayed the gritty, raw, rough and uncensored sex fantasy world of the dyke community in San Francisco. The film was nominated for three AVN awards, including Best All Girl Sex Scene. The film portrayed a variety of queer sexual dynamics and gender expressions including high femmes, daddies, butches and drag kings, and it blew the erotic minds of the mainstream adult industry. At the turn of the millennium, mainstream recognition for queer DIY porn was unheard of. SIR video really helped to put queer DIY porn on the map – leading the way for future generations of DIY porn makers, and giving us the push we needed to realize that yes, we could pick up the cameras ourselves, tell our own kinky queer stories without compromising who we were, and even get recognition and visibility within our industry.

Good Vibrations' early production imprint, Sex Positive Productions, led the way in documenting early millennial DIY porn with titles like *Slide Bi Me* (2001), *Voluptuous Vixens* (2002), *Whipsmart: A Good Vibrations Guide to Beginning S/M for Couples* (2002), and what ended up being my first full-length feature DVD as a performer, *G Marks the Spot: A Good Vibrations Guide to the G Spot* (2003). Good Vibrations films proved to us that porn could be both educational and entertaining. It showed us that we could smash stigmas and stereotypes while simultaneously representing individuals in a way that was authentic, and that celebrated the diversity of bodies, gender and pleasure.

DIY porn is not a new phenomenon, although it has gained greater traction in the past five years – specifically within the feminist and queer communities. *On Our Backs* was the first women-run erotica magazine, and the first magazine in the United States to feature lesbian erotica for a lesbian audience. *On Our Backs* released their first print magazine in 1984 and continued representing lesbian, dyke and queer sexuality up until 2006, when it ceased production. During that time, many of DIY queer porn's powerhouses and radical lesbian writers, artists and performers graced the pages of *OOB* and/or worked behind the scenes on the production of the magazine. The magazine was first founded in 1984 by sex educators Deborah Sundahl and Myrna Elana. Sundahl, along with Nan Kinney, spun off and created Fatale Video the following year, and by the late '80s became the largest producer of lesbian pornography in the world!

On Our Backs was an epic sexual archive of our queer culture with contributions by legends like Patrick Califia, Tee Corinne and Jewell Gomez. Future editors of the magazine included Susie Bright,

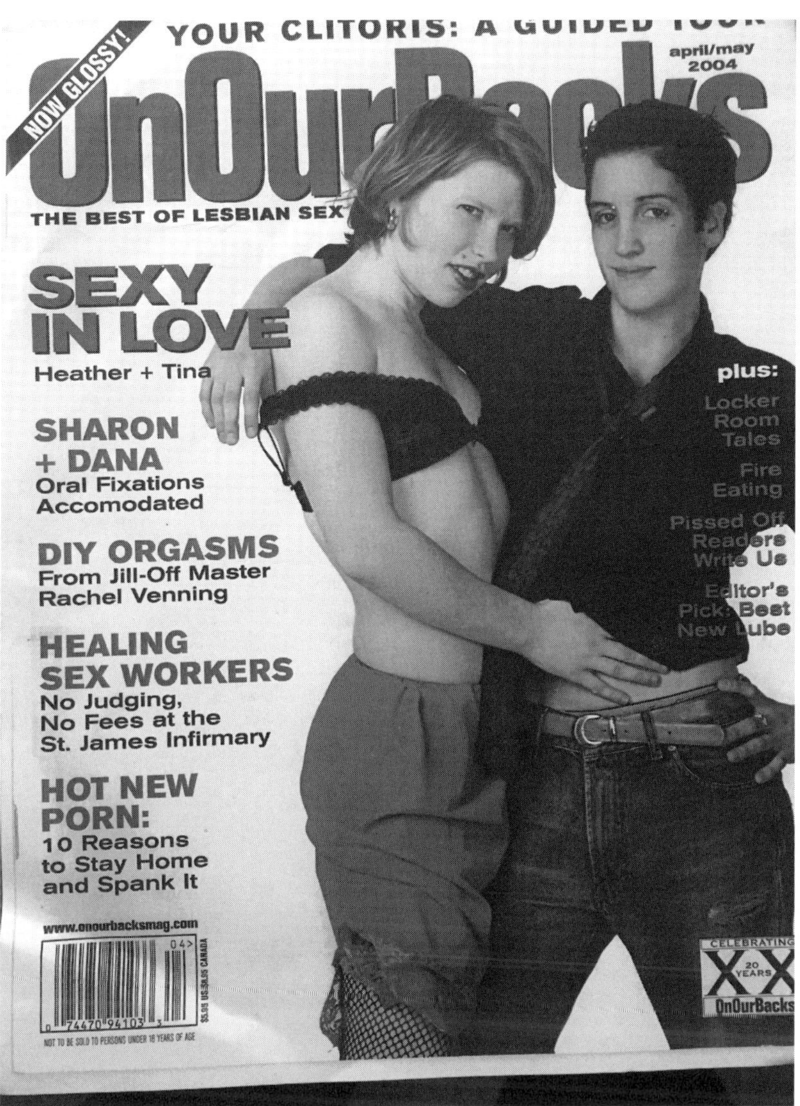

Diane Anderson-Minshall, Shar Rednour (of SIR Video), feminist porn icon Tristan Taormino and Diana Cage. In April of 2004, I graced the cover of *On Our Backs* with my girlfriend, for the first time appearing with them in a nude pictorial for the magazine, shot by erotic photographer Michael Rosen. *On Our Backs* portrayed queer sex the way that queers wanted to be represented, and we were doing it for ourselves. To see our sex lives and our culture portrayed in a way that felt honest and authentic was empowering, and validated our desires and relationships. These pages seemed to whisper in our ears with a confident and assertive voice, "We matter." And we listened, and we knew we weren't alone in our desire, or in our identities or our expressions of self.

It's important to realize that no one person orgasms the same way as another; no two people enjoy touch in exactly the same way. If we are able to document the diversity of ways in which we fuck, the ways we love, the ways we experience pleasure – these ways that are authentic to us and to our culture – then we empower all those who view our films. We empower them to explore their own sex lives and desires with confidence, and with the knowledge that we are all different. This provides the members of our culture with models for how to forge ahead in pursuit of their own pleasure.

In the process of holding space for authentic expressions of sexual pleasure, both the performer and the viewer are changed. The viewer is changed and empowered with a new perspective of what is possible. They have witnessed vulnerability, honesty – a primal, uncensored, unfiltered expression of self. The viewer has witnessed something intimate made public. They have been a spectator, perhaps for the first time, of raw human desire and connection. They have seen that desire can manifest in a myriad different ways when people embrace their humanness instead of attempting to hide it.

By this I mean witnessing bodies that are not airbrushed, not tanned to look thinner, not heavily made up. Each hair is not perfectly flat-ironed and enhanced with extensions, and no acrylic nails cover the humanness of our organic selves. This is not to say that these cosmetic alterations can't be a part of someone's authentic expression of self. But there is not just one way to express ourselves, our beauty or our desire, and our bodies or external shells don't need to fit into any one mold in order to express desire or be desirable.

Instead, within DIY porn, we see everyone – from real-life couples in their sixties to women and men in their twenties – negotiating how they like to have sex. We see a varied expression of gender, of sexual desire, and – again referring back to DIY culture – an ethos to make our own cultural voices heard: to speak up for and represent our own selves, because no one else will do it for us, and no one else can tell our stories with the same authenticity and passion.

Performers, crew, directors and producers are changed by the experience of creating DIY porn as well. And in a DIY production you might be simultaneously a performer, crew member, director and producer – that's how my first films were directed. Although it has its challenges, there is something wildly empowering about directing your own fantasies and living them out in front of the camera.

I remember my first experiences manifesting my fantasies on the camera. I had started modeling for Suicide Girls back in 2002 and found creative and artistic freedom working with photographers to express my own sexual vision and vantagepoint in front of the camera, which was encouraged by the Suicide Girl producers and photographers. My first photo set for Suicide Girls was an erotic portrait of myself and my electric guitar. At the time, I was a part of an experimental noise band called butcheR&smeaR, in which I played the electric guitar with my vibrator and drum sticks. Next was a series of photographs entitled SOIL – inspired by Carolee Schneemann's performance piece, *Interior Scroll* – in which I covered my body in a mound of dirt, unearthing from my vagina a scroll of text that I read aloud from atop a pedestal within my art gallery. I followed up those photos with a series of absurdist, vibrant, sploshing photographs, shot on film by renowned fetish photographer Charles Gatewood. This series married ideas of light and dark, humor and sex, grief and beauty, anxiety and release. I found it empowering to tell my own narratives in my own way, documenting and exploring my sexuality in a medium that felt natural to me. These experiences largely inspired me to pick up the camera and shoot my sexual journey on my own terms, for my own company.

As a director, I try to facilitate an empowering experience for other performers. For many women it's the first time they have had the opportunity to truly sculpt and take an active role in orchestrating their own sexual fantasies.

I recall my first introduction to performer and erotic media maker Tina Horn. My friend and colleague Lorelei Lee had introduced us, and Tina expressed an interest in performing in my films. I was impressed with the letter of introduction she sent to me. She was an artist and a writer, a punk and a feminist, and I had a feeling we would work well together. We met at the Break Room – a vegan coffeehouse in Oakland – and sat down to discuss her interest in feminist pornography and filmmaking. Over coffee and bagels, I told Tina about a film I was in preproduction for and was currently casting, called *LayOver.* A film inspired partially by *The Graduate* and partially by *Ice Storm*, two films set in the 1970s. Tina was over the moon with the idea, and I asked her what her fantasy scene would look like. She took a big drink of water, and with deep exhale revealed that her fantasy was to be a part of a double-penetration lesbian sex scene in which she was being fucked with strap-ons by two or three different women.

It is very rare that I get this kind of request for someone's cinematic debut, but I enthusiastically ensured Tina that we would make it happen. I started working on the script and casting with her to get the scene perfect. What was resulted was a very sexy '70s style "key party" that included Tina's fantasy double-penetration scene.

In my series *A Woman's POV* (Good Releasing), I invited the performers not only to reveal and live out their sexual fantasies on film, but turned the camera over to the them to capture their own orgasms, pleasure, ecstasy and desire, which showed in the very trembling of the camera. Performers were not only living their fantasies, but many were seeing for the first time themselves and their sexual arousal in real time through the viewfinder, as well as their partners' actions and reactions during their sexual connection. What resulted was an intimate and empowered experience, not only for the viewer but for the performer as well. Space was held for the individual to shift the pornographic narrative to the literal sexual gaze of the woman. The lens diverted to what she found arousing in her partner and it gave the audience a different perspective as we watched the

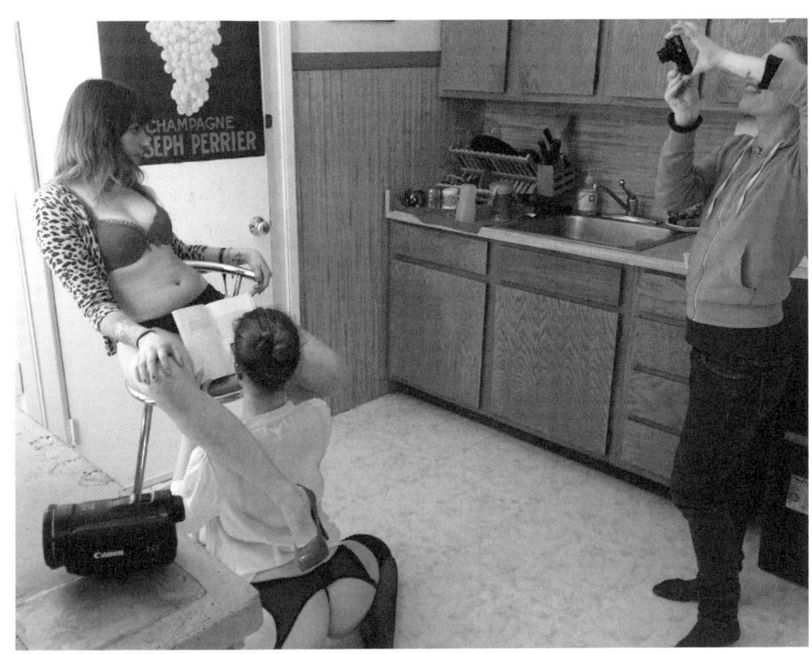

Missy Minks chose her partner for this scene in *Bibliophile,* and their chemistry and connection shows on film.

rise and fall of a chest, the trembling of a hand or leg, the curling of toes, and a partner's eyes gazing up at the lens as they beg to come.

Why is this important? Because our point of view, our perspective, our lives, our culture, our communities, matter. And these will not be lost or forgotten, or go undocumented because of societal shame that has been cast upon sexuality, queer sex and female sexuality. Rather than running away from difference, we are running towards it, embracing it with a queer lens and with the awareness that we are united in our human desire for love, affection and connection.

During a recent reading and Q&A I did in Sydney, Australia, after I had expounded upon the theoretical and sociopolitical aspects of feminist porn, a woman asked me, "But what does that look like when I'm looking at the screen? How do I look at a film and recognize feminist or DIY porn?"

My response was that DIY and feminist porn rely on a certain feminist and sex-positive ethos. They require an understanding of empowering our performers: presenting them with choices, and assisting in navigating an experience that feels authentic to the cast and represents who they are as individuals. Much of feminist and DIY porn emerges as a response to not finding a representation of the way we experience sexual pleasure in the films that we are watching. Filmmakers are motivated by feminist porn as a social movement, as a way to create social change and represent the sexual desires of the underrepresented. While the majority of mainstream porn is created with a purely commercial intent, feminist and DIY porn doubles as both art and activism. Erotic filmmaking is a unique undertaking in which filmmakers strive to create a social impact, and hopefully recoup costs. Like many artists, these filmmakers think out of the box in order to scrape together the funds they need to continue their practice and sustain themselves in their career.

So what does this look like on the screen? This might look like a couple negotiating the sex that they want to have – what turns them on and what toys they want to use. DIY porn might look like a simple shot of a person's hand as they reach for lubricant, or depict someone asking for lubricant during filming. DIY porn might look like safer sex supplies being used during filming, including shots of a condom, or footage of the condom going onto the cock or toy. DIY porn might look like discussion between partners during a scene, or eye contact, or ongoing communication throughout sex. DIY porn means that performers are wearing wardrobe that makes them feel hot, even if that doesn't fit the mold of traditional perceptions. You might not fully understand the beauty of boots or Converse tennis shoes, but if the performer feels hot in them, they are staying on. The performers are having the kind of sex that is hot to them, sex that they have chosen and that is negotiated with their scene partners both before and during the scene. It might feel like the sex is more intense or more connected because of these things being incorporated, but because feminist and DIY porn strives to honor the individual, each scene is individual, not formulaic – so each scene will differ in appearance and scenes will be as diverse as your cast of performers.

Why does feminist visibility in erotic film and pornography matter? Because we matter. Our sexual desire matters. It counts. We count. Our sexual culture matters – our relationships, fantasies, bodies, gender expression, struggles and successes. Every orgasm is radical. Every orgasm is its own revolution, creating change, screaming into the day or into the night, taking up space with radical love that has the ability to change the world.

Ignoring pornography, or simply condemning it when it doesn't tell our stories or portray sexual expression in a way that resonates with us, is not a forward-moving contribution to making our voices heard. In picking up the camera, we each have the power and ability to document and create narratives that are representative of how we experience sexual pleasure.

We must not forget that we still live in the shadow of scarlet letters. In a society that is shrouded in fear of our own bodies, our own pleasure, our own sex, our own porn and our own honest communication about our desires. This is a culture in which we still lack basic, inclusive sexual education. We live with everyday slut-shaming, body-shaming and catcalls that assault ears as we walk down the street. There is another way, and we do have the power and ability to disrupt and dismantle these fears and empower people with the ability to accept, embrace and communicate about who they are as sexual beings and who they want to be. The revolution won't be televised, but it will be filmed: the revolution is called DIY porn.

A CONVERSATION WITH MOM

"Well, some of what you do *is* a little bit shameful, Tina. I mean pornography is not really... well, it's... I wouldn't go telling the folks at work about it. It's so degrading." My mom's voice changed in tone. There were longer pauses between words and uncertainty and shame in the words that she was speaking. She was obviously having trouble speaking those words at all.

"Mom, porn is a really big genre of film. And you're right, some porn is degrading. Some sex that is not filmed is degrading too." This wasn't the first time that we'd had this conversation, and it wouldn't be the last. By now I knew how to speak with my mother about my career. I would suck the stigma out of the loaded conversation and make it as natural as swapping recipes.

"The way they talk about porn, you know, on television, like Jay Leno, he was making fun of porn. It's disgusting." Mom was still trying to back up her argument against pornography by referencing popular media.

"It's not all like that. I make feminist pornography. I listen to women and couples and they tell me their ultimate fantasies. And I create a safe space for them to play out those fantasies, and then document it. It's beautiful. I have couples who love each other, connecting deeply with each other and whispering that they love each other. It's amazing. It's really amazing. I feel privileged that they allow me to be present during such intimate moments." My eyes began to water as I became impassioned just speaking about my job.

"I understand, Tina. But why do you still have to use that word 'pornography'? That's not what people think of when they hear that word." My mother brought up a point that I'd heard many times before. If it's the documentation of sexual culture, is it truly porn, or is it something else entirely?

"Well, Mom, I'm going to be a part of that change."

4 STATING YOUR VALUES & VISION

WHY DID YOU DECIDE TO PICK UP THIS BOOK? WHAT WAS the vision, dream or brief moment of inspiration that led you to open these pages and delve deep into my inner workings?

Did you pick up this book and say, "I could do that. I could make an erotic film. The erotic films that I've seen out there lack quality (or are too formulaic or unreal or boring)"?

If those are the qualities of the films that don't resonate with you, I invite you to take three minutes to close your eyes and visualize a film that isn't formulaic, a film that isn't boring, a film that you would find hot, that would resonate with you and the way you experience desire and pleasure.

Notice what is happening, who is there, the emotional weather of the people having sex and your emotional weather as you watch them engage sexually. What relationships are evident?

Now invite those same characters into another environment – like a restaurant or café – and sit down with them in your vision. In this guided vision, I'd like for you to have a conversation with the performer, in which you explain to them how you feel about sexuality and pornography, and what your intentions are in creating erotic film.

What is the most important thing that you want to accomplish in the creation of your film? What values do you stand for? What will your film stand for? Speak honestly and openly with your characters, knowing that they are listening and believe in you, and that they want to support your vision. Speak with them knowing that you are collaborating to create something really beautiful and powerful.

Set a timer and give yourself a good five minutes for this conversation between the characters.

All right, now grab your journal. This journal is where your filmmaker exercises will live, and where you will jot down film ideas as they develop. You are a filmmaker, so take it seriously: give your ideas, your concepts, your films and your dreams a home.

What did the conversation with the characters in your vision look like? I want you to write for one minute – either free-form or more structured writing – about your values as they relate to erotic filmmaking.

Now pick up your pen and write for another minute about what your vision is, the impact you intend your filmmaking to have.

Some of you may have been thinking about this for a while, and already have your values and vision solidified. Some of you may be echoing values and vision of directors whom you know and admire. Try to define what is individual and authentic to you and the way that you see the world. Others might be unclear as to what direction you wish to pursue as a filmmaker and just what values they embrace.

I encourage you all to watch film if you plan on becoming a filmmaker. Watch film that inspires you. It doesn't have to be erotic or pornographic. Write about the elements of the film that are sexy and inspiring to you as an artist and a filmmaker. Then I want you to watch erotic film. Note what you like and don't like.

A wild abundance of feminist pornographers have come onto the scene within the last five years. The fabulous thing about this is that we have so many erotic filmmakers to discover: even I have trouble keeping up! There are annual erotic film festivals, films that are distributed online, and even our own annual awards show (www.feministpornawards.com)!

Some porn doesn't resonate with me. There is some feminist porn that I find just as boring as what I commonly refer to as "fast food porn" (or a formulaic commercial product, generated by the mainstream porn industry). However, there is plenty of feminist porn that does resonate with me, that I find inspiring and truly exciting. If you are looking for places to find what is currently out there, as well as to check out feminist porn of the past, numerous feminist porn studios and resources are listed at the back of this book. I highly recommend that you check them out. Research is an important element of creating relationships and community with other filmmakers and studios, as well as learning what inspires us in our own artistry.

Your vision statement is likely to change, shift and transform as you develop and change, learning more about yourself as a filmmaker. But let's start with the dream – the vision – and let it develop and change as we go. Your vision statement and values are something that you will constantly come back to in your practice as a filmmaker. When you are struggling with an idea, a concept for a film, casting or some other decision, you will return to your vision statement like the North Star – a constant that will keep you on your creative path and guide you through the exercise of achieving the impact that you desire.

Based on the above journal exercise, I'd like you to construct a formal Vision and Values Statement, which you can refer back to throughout your reading of this book.

Rock on! You are now a filmmaker who has a vision, and nothing is holding you back. You have a vision (Vision Statement) and you stand for something (Values Statement). It's time to create a vision board for your DIY porn production entity!

THE ANALOG VERSION

Grab some magazines (or print images from the web) and tear out images that embody the emotions and values you have solidified in your Vision and Values Statement. Now you have a visual to go with your words.

I also like to have an active "vision and inspiration board" online, in a blog format. You can use whatever platform is the most user-friendly for you. I really enjoy using wordpress.com, which is a free and easy-to-use blogging platform. I know other filmmakers and artists who find Pinterest an excellent resource for creating an online inspiration and vision board. Tumblr is another choice, and tends to be a more porn-friendly social media platform. With any of these platforms you can grab images, themes and memes that resonate with what you envision for your own film. Try to find images with commonality that point to a direction that your filmmaker self is attracted to.

As you develop and discover the look, feel and emotion that best inspires you in your work, you are also communicating the development of your work and the feelings, emotions and politics of your film to the public. This will come in handy, not only for your own creative development, but also for communicating to others the feel of the film that you are working to develop. This, along with your vision and values statements, will be key in developing and building a team for your production.

Last year I started directing and producing films for a new DIY porn producer, and worked with the company on solidifying their vision, values and policies for their art house film company. After reading the following Vision and Values statement, consider what you now know about this production company and what they hold to be important in their filmmaking. What are values that you share or that differ from this company? Often, examining other companies' vision and values can assist you in creating a platform to manifest your own vision, values and policies for production.

HELL BENT FILMS VISION STATEMENT

Hell Bent Films aims to produce cinematic works that cater to an erotic gaze which appeals to a primal human desire that obliterates any preconceived societal concepts of sex or gendered expectations. At Hell Bent Films, we are deconstructing sexual desire with intelligent connected passionate sexual experiences with in the context of fantastical, absurdist and iconic characters that exist in scenarios inspired by our favorite rock and art icons.

HELL BENT FILMS CODE OF ETHICS

Casting Policies, Protocol and Values – Hell Bent Films does not assume any cast or crew member's gender or pronouns, and will introduce all cast and crew in accordance with the name, gender and pronoun with which the cast or crew member communicates to the director.

Performers from any point of the gender spectrum will have an equal opportunity in the casting process.

Hell Bent Films values authentic on-screen sexual connection amongst our performers.

Performers' bodies and body hair are beautiful in their natural form, and at Hell Bent Film we honor and respect our performers' most natural expression of self - including whatever style or length of body hair a performer might choose to rock.

At Hell Bent Films we recognize that whatever a performer does with their body hair has absolutely no relevance to the scene and at no time will performers be asked to shave or grow body hair, or be discriminated against because of it. Because that's what Amanda Fucking Palmer would want!!!!!!

Cast and crew are treated with respect at all times. We are a team, collaborators, in art, in film, in radical porn. We recognize how important it is to support one another in the birth of a creative manifestation such as an epic art house film.

Smash the Hierarchy – All cast and crew members should be considered equals. We are all working together to make magic happen and everyone's role is key to a successful collaboration.

Our sets are not a place of gossip or judgment. We celebrate the diversity and beauty of our experiences and desire and will not tolerate racist, sexist, homophobic, transphobic or offensive language on our set.

In order to advocate for and accurately represent performers' voices, desires and opinions, pre-scene and/or post-scene interviews will be conducted.

PORNOGRAPHY AS PROTEST: DIRECT ACTION AND DIY PORN, BY ZAHRA STARDUST

Zahra Zsuzsanna Stardust is an Australian artist and scholar who writes and practices in explorations of the body, pleasure and labor. Using her body as a canvas, her work employs queer intimacies and radical politics to examine sexuality, gender and regulation. Her award-winning work has been screened, exhibited, workshopped and performed across several continents, and her writing appears in academic books and journals.

I had zero experience in film production when I started making DIY porn. Everything I learned was by observation, skill-share and trial and error.

Outrage at injustice brought me to DIY porn. In my decade-long stripper career, a few things happened. My inner labia were airbrushed in a softcore magazine to meet Classification requirements that genitals be "discreet." My armpit hair was edited out by a photographer before photos were sent for publication. My piercings were mysteriously removed from the cover of a national magazine.

Around the same time, Australian Customs banned any import of films featuring g-spot ejaculation (believing it was urination, constituting fetish, and therefore banned). The Classification Board instructed trainees that women with small breasts may be seen as "underdeveloped" and therefore be "refused classification" (for appearing under eighteen). Fisting, bondage, candle wax and even spanking were unlawful to depict.

Meanwhile, porn appealed to me as a way to explore the thresholds of my body. I sought pleasure in radical acts of intimacy and joy in the creative process. I wanted to contribute to a community, movement and body of work with broader significance. I wanted to make DIY porn.

The trouble was, the industry in Australia was so tiny. I was thrilled to perform with two "erotica" companies until one was prosecuted and relocated to Amsterdam. There were no blueprints, no infrastructure, no thriving industry. We had to take things into our own hands.

I started getting involved in artistic collaborations blending sex and politics. I had my pink bits photographed to showcase vulva diversity. One art collaboration was banned from a gallery, another nude demonstration moved on by police.

I asked my fellow tutor in Gender Studies to film me masturbating with a handycam in my ex's garage. We borrowed a fucking machine from a couple I met at a rope workshop. We filmed cute things like crushing strawberries in red stilettos and experiments with soy cream. I insisted my then-girlfriend break into an abandoned warehouse before it was bulldozed, to film me fucking myself in the toilet cubicles. A pole dancing friend donated two boxes of Barbie Dolls from storage towards a photo set for *Slit* magazine, which involved us using Barbie as a dildo. Barbie came in handy later for our film *Fuck Dolls,* where we inserted her headfirst into a strap-on harness.

I spent hours home alone with a borrowed camera, gleefully devising the best angle to film myself squirting, entertaining myself with filters and cross-fades, editing around blurry footage and searching for the cords to convert film to digital. Stripping had taught me the art of reveal, musicality and pacing. My initial edits looked shamelessly amateurish and I didn't care. I found the whole process just fabulous.

My first short film was called *Beautiful Monotony*, about blurred boundaries between work and pleasure. I put out a Facebook call for free lap dances and friends kindly lined up early one morning for a three-hour endurance montage of lap dances, edited it in fast-forward, interspersed with scenes of studying, eating and counting cash.

When national current affairs program *QnA* featured anti-porn feminists remarking that the "one on the bottom" was "oppressed" in gay porn, my then-partner and I naturally responded with a hardcore sex film called *The One on the Bottom*. With one hand filming and the other fisting, we juxtaposed political commentary alongside gushes of unrepentant grrrl juice.

Many other films and trades-for-content were birthed over vegan meals, festival workshops, Skype dates and herbal tea. I became obsessed with body fluids. My boifriend reached inside me for bloody tampons, squeezed them into my mouth, and I tweeted the pics on #livetweetyourperiod. He helped collect my ejaculate for bottling in a Bent Art exhibition. When Courtney Trouble came down under, we made a hot wet mess to subvert the conventional "cum shot" and called it *Femme Facial*.

DIY porn is protest. It challenges government intervention into our lives, the heteronormative reproductive agenda, and what sexual intimacies are considered obscene. Those of us who are making DIY porn are doing so as an act of civil disobedience, because we know from lived experience that the cost of censorship in our communities is too high.

Laws prohibiting depiction of fisting, ejaculation or BDSM actively produce a heterosexist, misogynist sexuality as "normal," while pathologizing intimacies that can be life-affirming, consensual and meaningful.

In a criminalized environment, where our bodies, desires and sexualities are deemed "offensive," DIY porn is protest. DIY porn becomes a form of insubordination, a symbolic violation of laws designed to closet and invisiblise us. When we are excluded from participation in law reform, porn becomes our protest mechanism. DIY porn becomes an act of nonviolent resistance.

As classification becomes redundant in an age of convergent media, community standards are now being determined by corporations. Billing companies preclude menstrual porn, social media removes breastfeeding photos, crowdfunding sites tax adult campaigns, video platforms take down sexual content – with little consistency, transparency or recourse.

When we Do it Ourselves, we take control of the means of production. Our representations are not mediated by third parties, "experts" or "professionals" wanting to pathologize us, speak for us, or profit from us. In DIY porn, we are not models in someone else's project, but authors of our own experience.

DIY Porn is about redistribution of wealth. When we self-fund, self-publish and self-determine, we enjoy political autonomy that is not compromised by donors, investors or markets. DIY porn says fuck you to production values that are only about class and keeping porn elite. DIY porn is for everybody – it can be filmed on your phone, in your home, by your friend. We can dilute hegemonic representations through user generated porn.

Lastly, DIY porn is a form of political communication. It speaks to democracy, representation and access to decision-making. It is an exercise in community building, not an individualist pursuit. When we build from the ground up, not the top down, when we share resources, knowledge and skills, we can create stronger, mobilized and empowered communities.

In Australia, the number of DIY porn producers now surpasses the number of mainstream producers. We keep fucking, keep loving, keep Doing It Ourselves.

5 SPACE TO BE INSPIRED

IN ORDER TO DISCOVER WHAT TURNS US ON AND WHAT we desire, we must first be comfortable and feel safe in exploring our options. Many people yearn for and desire a wide variety of intimate touch.

As the person who will be holding space for and documenting a wide variety of different sexual fantasies, it's important to understand desire. We are all different. We all have a desire for different sexual flavors. That's part of what makes us fabulous and diverse. Below I've listed some different sexual acts and fetishes that some people enjoy.

You don't have to share the same fetish or desire as another person. But if you understand and hold space for the authentic expression of that desire, and make room to learn more about it, then you are facilitating space for others to also learn about the way this individual authentically expresses their sexual desire when given the space to do so. As a teacher once told her students, "We don't yuck someone else's yum."

Read the list below and make stars next to fetishes and sexual acts that you desire either in real life, fantasy or films that you watch.

- ☐ Threesomes
- ☐ Double Penetration
- ☐ Orgies
- ☐ Kink
- ☐ Sadism/Masochism
- ☐ Role Play
- ☐ Sploshing
- ☐ Cake Sitting
- ☐ Fisting
- ☐ Spanking
- ☐ Enemas
- ☐ Anal play
- ☐ Public Sex
- ☐ Sex in Nature
- ☐ Rope Bondage
- ☐ Fetishes: foot fetish, shoe fetish, leather fetish, latex fetish
- ☐ Squirting
- ☐ Sex in Water
- ☐ Balloon Fetish
- ☐ Panty Fetish

◆

As a young woman, performing in erotic film was a place I found that was safe for me to explore who I was as a sexual person. It gave me a clear communication platform in which to negotiate what my desires were. I knew what looked hot to me in films that I watched.

I knew what images ran through my mind when I was fantasizing in bed and wet between my legs, but I didn't know until I started exploring sex in practice what felt good and what I wanted more of.

I was hungry for sensation and fearless in trying every chocolate in the box. Some of the flavors may have sounded a little strange at first, but I didn't allow that to deter me from trying them out and seeing, for example, what the physical sensations and emotional experience might be like of being tied upside down to a water fountain in Mexico, or tied spread-eagle to a Jeep as it drove through the jungle, or fisted on a rooftop in Manhattan, or having trifle and pies thrown at my naked quivering body in London.

I said "yes" to these experiences, and I explored the really kinky desires that weren't necessarily my cup of tea but that I understood. I understood the release, the part of the mind and body that found control or pleasure or catharsis in the exploration of different fetishes – like sploshing (the act of getting messy with food or gooey materials for erotic pleasure), golden showers (having someone pee on to your body or peeing on someone else's body as erotic play), and enemas (inserting fluids – like water or milk – into the anus, and expelling them).

When we set aside our judgment and don't automatically "yuck someone's yum," we can start to understand it, understand them, and understand our universal commonality of desire. We can hold space for those desires to be further explored and expressed in an authentic and diverse manner.

LET'S HAVE A WRITING-GASM!

Okay, it's time to get writing! I'd like for you to write out a conversation with your desire. This is an exercise in which we personify our desire and kindly, compassionately, without judgment, listen to what it wants. Ask your desire what it wants, what it lusts for. Listen to your desire. Do not judge or censor the voice of your desire. Follow the conversation, asking desire more detailed questions about moments in its existence in which it felt satiated or inspired. Have it describe those moments.

An example might look like this:

Me: Hello, Desire.

Desire: Hello.

Me: I wanted to ask you a question.

Desire: Go for it. I'm waiting.

Me: Well, what do you lust for? What really turns you on?

Desire: I want to be full.

Me: Full?

Desire: I want to be so full of cock. I want cock stuffed down my throat, in my cunt, and two cocks rubbing against one another that pump in and out of my ass. I want to be so full.

Me: Wow! Tell me more about that. Where are you when you are full of all of these cocks?

Desire: Somewhere filthy. Maybe a garage. Maybe they're mechanics covered in oil and dirt. Everything is just so dirty and it feels so good, my sweat mixed with the dirt.

Set your timer for five minutes. Let your desire just talk. And really listen, don't judge. Affirm, and ask questions that give room for your desire to reveal more of itself to you. Discovering and becoming comfortable with your own desire will aid you in better facilitating space for others to express their desire as well. This also might aid you in discovering what type of scenes you might be the most interested in directing, or directing and performing in.

Although it might be super exciting to unearth discoveries about your own personal desire, if you are not the performer in a film, you will actually need to try to contain your personal desires. Remember that as a director, you are creating and holding space for the exploration and expression of the performers' authentic sexualities, not projecting your own experience onto the performers. Even if you create a narrative based on your own personal desires, try to create space for the performers to make the roles and exploration of those desires their own, rather than overwhelming them with your own personal experiences.

FILM-GASMS

Take a moment to think about the hottest moment that you remember from a mainstream film. Go find that film and re-watch it. Really take note of what elements of the film – what specific shots – turned you on the most. Was it dialogue? A sex scene? An action scene? A scenario? What feelings did it evoke? Freeze frame the film at the shots in the movie that you found the hottest, and take a photo or screen grab of the film at that shot. Collect all the shots that were the most exciting to you. Look at these and delve into why they may have been sexy to you. Are they still sexy to you? If not, what current films really capture an element of sexual desire that resonates with you? Watch those films and explore the shots that construct those lustful moments for you.

6 BUILDING COMMUNITY

WHEN I CAME INTO DIRECTING DIY PORN, I HAD ALREADY established a community in the Bay Area, as a curator of artistic programming for my gallery and within the feminist porn world as a porn performer. I had been building relationships with artists, performers and directors for about five years before I picked up the camera and started directing my own films. I had the advantage of discovering directors and performers I really enjoyed working with, and with whom I shared the same political vision and sex-positive ethos.

When I discovered that I felt connection and excitement working with a fellow performer or crew member on another director's set, I was able to network on that set and tell them about my vision for my own directorial work, to gauge whether they had interest in working on one of my projects.

When I modeled for a director who was creating work that I admired and resonated with, I made sure to find ways to cross-pollinate, promoting their work or including them in film screenings, festivals or events that I was programming. Many of the interns and volunteers at my gallery watched my films and asked to perform in them, as they were interested in erotic film and wanted to explore their fantasies with someone they knew and trusted. They became really familiar with my work by attending screenings and taking on photographer or production assistant gigs when they were available. I would hire my friends with graphic design skills to make my box covers, promotional materials, logos and business cards. There was a lot of cross-pollination between the feminist art community that I was already a part of and the DIY porn community that I was building. What communities are you already connected with, and how do you feel they would receive your vision for DIY porn making?

An important element of networking and connecting with your allies and community is knowing how to talk about your work with confidence. Practice talking about why you believe in your work and DIY porn – first in front of a mirror and then with a supportive friend. People respond to fearless passion; they want to be a part of something that is exciting, and what you are venturing into is something brave and exciting that has the ability to help shape the way people communicate and perceive sex. Make sure always to have a business card with you: you never know when you're going to meet someone who will be the next great addition to your team.

After knowing how to speak authentically and with confidence about your work, the key is to listen. Listen to what other people are passionate about. Are they passionate about photography, web design, sound engineering, playing the violin, social media? Make note of what they do, get their contact information, and remember them as you are creating a project. Every time you meet someone, you are expanding your network and creating space and opportunity for yourself and others to live out their dreams.

There are certain places that you might find more liberal, open attitudes around sex, sexuality and pornography. Some cities are going to be more accepting and supportive than others. You probably already have a gauge of how conservative or accepting your city might be. I grew up in Southern Ohio outside of Cincinnati. When

For the premiere of *The StarrLust Experience,* the cast, crew and even the audience dressed up as the characters from the film.

I read from my kinky memoir *Daddy* in Cincinnati last winter, one couple walked out. I was a bit surprised there weren't more! I also know that certain areas of my conservative hometown were more conservative than others. Clifton was a little liberal-ish pocket where you would find a few punks with mohawks, an art house theater and some indie rock shows. Find the communities that are embracing alternative cultures and alternative ways of viewing bodies, art, film and sexuality.

If I were holding a presentation on feminist porn or an erotic film screening in Southern Ohio, I would probably try to connect with other existing alternative subcultures in the area. For example, punk culture and body modification communities, as well as LGBTQ, feminist and kink communities, might be more receptive to DIY porn. Many cities have monthly kink munches, feminist meetups or groups at colleges, and LGBTQ groups, bars and cafes. These can be great leads in connecting with allies and communities with whom you might want to collaborate or reach out to in your filmmaking process.

Often you can reach out to these groups via email and introduce yourself and your work. Write to the group briefly about why your vision is important and why you believe they should know about your work, or the ideas you have about collaborating with their group.

Colleges are great for sourcing film students to act as production assistants, editors and videographers. Many of them, if they are in college, can actually borrow equipment from the school for outside projects. Just make sure that all crew and cast are over eighteen; check IDs at the interview. I generally try not to work with anyone who is under twenty, because that is my personal comfort level. All cast and crew also need to have two U.S. government-issued IDs such as a state id, drivers license, passport, or military id.

So all the above ways to connect are in-person ways to get out there and build your network. I do believe that face-to-face sharing of your passion and vision is key, but one of the cool things about our digital age is that you can also connect and build your network through social media and web presence.

Some basic ways of doing this are to start a blog site just for your film work. You can start one super easily and for free at sites like Wordpress.com. In fact, I start a new Wordpress site for each film, book or major project I take on. It takes an hour or less to start one and it's a great calling card for your vision.

If you decide to make use of social media, you can make a lot of initial contacts with other filmmakers, performers, crew and more, through media outlets like Facebook, Tumblr and Twitter. Indie porn producers and performers are very accessible through social media, so discover what filmmakers you like within the erotic film world, watch their films, and then reach out to them through social media. Ask us questions. We are passionate about our work just like you are, and love to help budding new filmmakers however we can.

Also, if you are able to take a few months off from a job, contact one of your favorite filmmakers and see if they have any internships at their company. Interning for a filmmaker is one of the best ways to observe and learn how an artist works. Keep collaborating, keep asking, keep seeking and keep dreaming.

Once you have identified who your allies are, how do you connect with them?

Some of my allies are collaborators I simply reached out to by email. I first met Shine Louise Houston of Pink and White Productions while curating her paintings at my art gallery, and we started talking about the film company she was starting. Shine ended up working on the crew of a Tony Comstock film I was cast in, so she got to see me performing. She then cast me in her initial demo reel that she used to pitch her epic queer porn film, *The Crash Pad.*

Back in 2003, I reached out to one of my heroes – now a friend and longtime collaborator – Carol Queen, by emailing a request to interview her for Suicide Girls, which was a website I had modeled for. Many models have first reached out to me via email or social media, showing interest and indicating that my vision and work resonated with them.

Although email and social media can be an excellent way to start the conversation between yourself and a performer or crew member, don't underestimate the importance of a face-to-face conversation. You want to make sure that your chemistry, values and collaborative dynamic are going to work. Don't compromise your vision or ethos in order to cast or hire "someone." You don't just want "someone." This film is your baby. You want to find the right someones to be on your team.

ORGANIZING AN ART EXHIBITION VS. ORGANIZING A DIY PORN FILM

When I'm curating an art event, I'm assembling a group of people to make art. I need to make sure that the artists are going to complement one another, that they will work well together, that all of our politics and visions are aligned. I hold space and facilitate the flow of each individual performance, or the curation of each artist, but give room for the individual artists to breathe life, authenticity and personal truth into their performance, their art.

It's the same process with directing a porn, but there are multiple levels of curation: the curation of the performers on set within their scene; the curation of the videographer and photographer associated with the choice of shots, audio and imagery to be captured on film; and the final curation occurring within post-production, encompassing the curation of each captured image within the editing process.

Having knowledge of all three levels of curation as the action is happening is a skill that takes time and experience for a director to develop. Although reading this handbook will certainly give you a leg up in your DIY filmmaking experience, it's when you pick up the camera and delve into the filmmaking process that you will start to develop muscles, and new levels of consciousness, in relation to manifesting your vision.

So get your hands messy! Start exploring and experimenting. Even if you have an editor and videographer, I highly recommend that you take on some small projects to learn editing and video. Learning all aspects of filmmaking gives you a greater understanding and a more nuanced language to use in communicating your vision to your crew. It also helps you to develop those three-level curatorial muscles.

TOP 3 TIPS FOR BUILDING DIY PORN COMMUNITY

1. Be fearless and confident in your vision and able to communicate that vision to a variety of communities.
2. Identify groups within your local, national and global communities that might share your vision. Connect with local groups in person whenever possible, and with national and global communities at conferences and film festivals.
3. Reach out to fellow filmmakers online as resources, and develop your own online presence and vision through blogs and social media.

My first step in organizing a porn production (after writing the script and securing funding, which we will get to in a later chapter) is building my team. This is where all that networking and listening to who is passionate about what comes in handy. If my film is specific to a certain location, like a coffee shop, gallery or bar that a friend owns, I call or email the location to see when they might be available. Hopefully this is a location that you already have a relationship with, and that already knows about your work because of your awesome networking skills. But don't be afraid to ask at venues and locations that you don't know. If they say yes, then you have expanded your network, and if they say no, then you move on to the next location or new idea. If I've noticed that another erotic film was shot at a certain location, then I know that the location is at least open to the idea of an erotic film being shot there, and I might have a better chance of that venue saying yes.

I was once shooting a film – *Lesbian Life: Real Sex NYC* – in New York, and I was looking for a diner location. I noticed in one of Joanna Angel's films for her porn production company Burning Angel, that Joanna had shot at Food Swings – a Brooklyn-based

I shot this scene of Nic and Jess first thing in the morning after getting off of a cross country red eye flight. No rest for the wicked. We shot the scene at one of my favorite vegan diners in Brooklyn - Food Swings.

vegan diner that I had frequented during my travels to New York. I called and emailed the diner about my film, and they were very excited to have me shoot there.

We did run into some challenges at that location, mainly with sound. Diners and cafes, although they look cool, often don't have the best lighting for film and often have a lot of audio buzz. We had turned off most of the electronics, but the freezer and fridge couldn't be turned off for risk of damaging the food.

Usually if I'm shooting at a house in a kitchen or anywhere near the kitchen, I unplug the fridge. A trick I learned to help me remember to plug the fridge back in is to put your car keys in the fridge. That way before you leave, you will have to go back to the fridge, realize it's still unplugged and plug it back in.

Shooting at the vegan diner proved to be humorous and a little problematic, in more ways than one. You know that old trope about the deliveryman arriving on the porn set and then joining in on the fun? Well, our delivery person didn't join in, but we did get interrupted a couple times. It was a humorous sight to have two queers boning in the diner with strap-ons and watch the deliveryman walk in with the organic veggies.

There was also a sous chef in the kitchen prepping lunch specials and chopping veggies while the scene was being shot in the front dining area. During all those slightly humorous moments, my most important job, even more than getting the shot, was making sure the performers felt safe, secure and supported. It is most important for me to let the performers know that I'm advocating for them over any particular shot. Because ultimately if the performers are not feeling comfortable and connected in the scene, the film will suffer and your vision and team will fail.

After I have booked a venue, I start to put together my team. I contact my crew, which varies depending on the budget and my needs for the film, but generally consists of a videographer, photographer, production assistant and sometimes a makeup artist. These are some of the key roles you want to be looking for when you are networking within your allied communities.

Regarding performers, after years in the industry I usually have certain performers in mind for a film project, but if you are contacting people for the first time you might want to put together a casting call. You can post this on your blog and social media accounts, as well as reach out via social media to performers and directors whose work resonates with you or who you think would pair well with your project. Shoot for the moon and you will land amongst the stars. Where do you think you will find the community of folks both interested in viewing and performing in your film? What events, club nights, bars or venues would your audience and cast frequent? Ask coordinators of those events if you can make a quick announcement about your film, or post a flyer for your casting call at venues and events you think might attract the cast you are looking for. Maybe a queer cabaret, a burlesque event or a nude art drawing class is where you want to post your casting call. I've included a casting call below from a film that I performed in for the feminist porn director Jincey Lumpkin, as an example of what you might want to include in your own casting call.

Single White Femme, LLC is on the lookout for sexy women to star in a hot new project called *Taxi*, shooting in New York City in July.

CONCEPT: In the back of one New York City taxi, eleven women experience the most sensual encounters of their lives. Directed by internationally acclaimed fashion photographer Diana Scheunemann (www.dianascheunemann.com), *Taxi* will be the first in a series of erotic short films produced by Jincey Lumpkin, Esq., for her brand-new, membership-based, streaming erotic video site, launching in September. We're making luxury lesbian pornography for the American Apparel generation.

	Movie sex, but hardcore and without the story! Join the revolution.
LOOK:	Shadowy, retro, cinematic, inspired by steamy classic European films.
DATES:	Shoot is scheduled July 6-12.
STARRING:	So far, a few vets and some new faces, too – Jiz Lee, Syd Blankovich, Madison Young, Dallas, Nic and Sir Sterling.
SEEKING:	We're still looking for the following roles:
	- 2 Femme gals to play in a "first time scene"
	- 1 edgy Femme to play a dominatrix and get down and dirty in a rough way
	- 2 Femmes comfortable with strap-on play
COMPENSATION:	We will pay travel, lodging and the customary rate for lesbian scenes. If you live outside of New York, we will pay for travel and lodging.

Be a part of the glitter and glam that will soon be streaming from the computer screen. Contact the project's producer, Jincey Lumpkin, Esq., if interested.

I've organized a lot of films over the years, and what I've noticed is that the most memorable projects for me to work on are the ones that are the most personal. The second film I wrote and directed, *Tail of A Bondage Model*, was a film that was very personal to me; much of the script was pulled directly from a memoir of the same name that I was working on at that time.

The film included narrative around my falling in love with someone outside of the porn world, her struggles with my constant traveling for work, and the jealousy that was aroused by the sexual nature of my work. The film also dove into our breakup, and my relationship with rope and with a new partner. The film explored some really difficult emotions and scenes for me, revealing eroticism as well as a very intimate and vulnerable self.

As an artist and filmmaker, I document and process my experiences in front of the camera. The films I create become containers, holding within them intimate sexual experiences and discoveries, a trace of my sexual evolution projected onto the screen.

I was screening a clip from my film *Art House Sluts* at a presentation I gave entitled "Intersections Between Performance Art and Queer Porn," at Grace Exhibition Space – a performance art gallery in Brooklyn. One scene featured the performance art duo Twincest, consisting of Jiz Lee and Syd Blakovich. The piece encompassed both explicit sex and performance art, as they snipped off hair from long blonde wigs they were both wearing, cutting away this pornographic trope and image to reveal their raw queerness underneath. They proceeded to engage in carnal sex utilizing lunch meat as props – fellating hot dogs and using deli sliced turkey as dental dams – referencing Carolee Schneemann's 1970s feminist performance piece *Meat Joy.*

The orgasmic climax to their scene concluded with Jiz Lee standing over Syd's naked body ejaculating into Syd's mouth and spitting a fountain of Campbell's tomato soup onto Syd's face – a sex act we coined "the Warhol." The duo then stood up and bowed to the audience of onlookers that included an Andy Warhol-like character played by Sadie Lune, and an Edie Sedgwick character.

One of the audience members at the screening asked me, "Are we supposed to feel turned on by this scene? Isn't that the purpose and intent of pornography?"

And my answer was: "No, not always. My goal for the performers and for the viewer is not based or focused on orgasm or arousal. Instead my focus lies in creating film that explores sexuality, identity and sexual expression of self. I want for my audience to feel:

sadness, loss, humor, pleasure, confusion, anxiety, tension and emotional release."

Much like performance art, pornography is a visceral, primal, outward, body-based expression of emotion. Often we actors, in both performance art and pornography, find ourselves coming up close to strong expressions of self – being released from our fleshy containers while our bodies are pushing to find their limits, their edges. Simultaneously these experiences are being publicly witnessed.

I try to create work that represents the complexity of life and our relationship with our bodies, desire, identity and sexual expression. My hope is that my films create space for conversations around sex and desire, and that they expand our ideas of what sexual desire might look like: that we can explore a full range of emotions as a catalyst for our sexual relationships with ourselves and others.

What is the intent of your films? What emotions and conversations do you hope to evoke through your filmmaking? What communities will you build in the creation of this work and through its screenings?

TRICKS OF THE TRADE, BY JIZ LEE

Jiz Lee is a porn performer, an industry outsider insider, and a wearer of many hats. They would like to thank: Andre Shakti, Arabelle Raphael, Bella Vendetta, Danny Wylde, James Darling, James Deen, Jimmy Broadway, Kelly Shibari, Kimberly Kane, Lorelei Mission, Mickey Mod, Ms. Naughty, Owen Gray, Siri, Stoya, and Tobi Hill-Meyer. Now go buy their shit. This piece was originally published on PinkLabel.tv.

"Didn't you shoot a scene with her? When's the video going to come out?"

Whenever the topic comes up, my porno candle dims a little. This summer marks the second anniversary of one of the hottest performances of my career, and I'm beginning to think the video will never be released. Even worse, I have no one to blame but myself.

Don't get me wrong; despite that sloppy mistake, I have had success. With all great things, there was definitely a learning curve. *Justify My Jiz* (with Wolf Hudson) is one positive example that taught me the long-term financial benefits of shared content. Where a paid shoot only offers a one-time check, owning the rights and revenue of the video on PinkLabel.tv has brought me a steady stream, month after month. I also witnessed how trades can equally benefit new producers. (Our shoot was one of many to help him establish WolfHudsonisBad.com.)

These days, porn performers don't have to depend solely on being booked with established companies. As the effects of Measure B and online piracy impede major studio productions, some industry trends see performers subsidizing their careers with cam shows, custom videos, Clips4Sale studios, and launching their own member sites. Equipment and web technology is becoming increasingly accessible. Performers of any notoriety can grab a camera and do it themselves. You scratch my back; I'll scratch yours.

Looking to learn from my embarrassing mistakes and gain 'best-practice' knowledge for the next time, I did what I should have done years ago: I decided to ask around.

TRADE VS SHARE... VS...

Producer, director and performer Jimmy Broadway details three types of non-paid content deals: Shared ("where both parties have full and equal use of the content"); Trade or "one-for-one" ("where I shoot a scene for you and you shoot a scene for me"); and Barter for Services ("where I provide camera, lighting, or location for your scene in exchange for getting you as talent for mine").

With each option, it helps to think outside the box, creating deals that fit individual needs. Multi-talented (and upcoming 2015 XBiz Awards host) James Deen points out "that compensation can come in many forms other than monetary value." On the other end of the "James-spectrum," indie porn star James Darling informs me that he's done trades in exchange for expensive toys and fetish gear. And while not a trade, *per se,* beloved porn star and sapient author Stoya notes a performer tie-in to commercial royalties from her Fleshlight masturbation sleeve (aptly named "Stoya Destroya"). With many different ways to compensate participants, there seems to be a potential for fair deals for everyone within the industry.

A QUESTION OF ETHICS

Siri opened her Clip4Sale store in 2012, before launching SIRIpornstar.com last year, primarily working with content shares. As a performer, she'll occasionally do a content trade when it's a unique shoot that she wants to own exclusively. She also brings up one of the big ethical concerns I have when watching emerging performers trade with producers of established sites.

"I don't share or trade content with people who have much larger methods of distribution than my own – that would create a really wide gap between our profit margins, which I believe is unfair," says Siri. "That's why even though I've been approached for content share/trade by directors before, I've never agreed to any content sharing/trading with producers who regularly can afford to hire talent for a scene – they would profit from the scene exponentially more than I would."

Siri also warns performers to beware of signs that they could be taken advantage of, and advocates for their autonomy in doing the scenes they want to do. Deals should be equally beneficial to both parties. "Look out for anyone who seems like they're trying to convince you that you should share content with them, because if they have to do any convincing they're probably aware that they're kind of taking advantage of you, or that they will benefit more from it in some way." As with paid scenes, performers should be comfortable declining a shoot for any reason. "You're working for free, because you hope to profit from the content, so you should be 100% sure that you will love doing the work!"

When I asked Stoya about trade ethics, she was quick to point out that "even paid work can be imbalanced with the worker getting the short end of the stick." Perhaps trade opportunities can offer the potential for a more level playing field.

THE GAME PLAN

Across the board, the most repeated advice I heard was always to come prepared. Performer Mickey Mod paints the big picture: "Never underestimate the value of pre-production. Have a plan, not just for the content, but also for the delivery of the finished product." Seems simple enough, yet this is often overlooked, as many performers may not have what it takes to shine on both sides of the camera.

Performer Danny Wylde didn't enter the porn industry with a desire to become a producer. He says that although the thought of expanding a market and making income upfront can be tempting, it's not for everyone. He's witnessed new performers with loose plans to start their own website or line of films fail because they didn't realize how much work goes into producing content. "It seems to fall apart more often than not," he notices. "I don't think many young performers understand that producing content is a full-time job, and not just something you do on the side for extra money. Of course, there are webmasters who will supply services for you at no upfront cost. But they typically take such a large percentage that it's not worth the effort." It's important to keep in mind that even working for free comes with a price, including paying third party help, hosting, and other hidden costs.

Perhaps some can balance the difference, if they have a clear trajectory. Arabelle Raphael got her start modeling by doing trade for content to build a portfolio, began performing for companies like Burning Angel, and has recently begun performing with other models doing both shares and trades for her Clips4Sale studio, Arabelle's Busty Playground. I was visiting Raphael's home the day she got her first studio check in the mail. "It's a great way for individual performers to make and distribute their own content," she says, adding that if given the option to do a trade or paid shoot she would not do trade unless the content was special.

"There's something to be said for just accumulating content for the sake of accumulating content," reasons burlesque dancer and porn performer Andre Shakti. "Maybe you have a 'five year plan' of starting a membership site, or a vague idea that you'll want this material for 'something' in the future, you're just not sure what – but if that's the case, then make sure you're prepared to put out a lot of money while you're in limbo." Shakti recently launched her website AndreShaktiXXX.com, and is strategizing to see returns.

To call Kimberly Kane an "established" porn star is an understatement. The multi-award winning adult actress and director has taken hold of her own content by storm. While she sees a lot of value in other big names trading content, she cautions new performers who are just starting out and suggests they do trades only when they are close to launching a website or Clips4Sale studio. "An established performer will already have many ways to distribute the content quickly." She strives to get her content everywhere and advises others do the same: "Try to eventually have a personal website, Clips4Sale studio, VOD, and DVD distribution deal." Be ready to hit the ground running.

The advice comes from lessons learned. Kane readily shares her past hurdles that include "having a website but not shooting enough to keep my members happy. And not having enough ways to distribute my content to get it to the maximum amount of potential buyers."

Other pitfalls? Another common piece of advice is to always keep things professional. A clearly written contract, even among close friends, trumps a casual attitude of assumed agreements. BBW star Kelly Shibari stressed that things be kept strictly business. "I think the most important thing is to make sure you're working with a reputable producer or other model, and to make sure that everyone involved understands the trade shoot as a non-personal, business-only transaction." Mickey Mod nails it: "Bad trades can ruin friendships."

5 STEPS TO PREPARE BEFORE THE SHOOT

1. *Pick your partners wisely.* Do thorough research on your scene partner to ensure the trade is worth your while. A passionate and intimate performer, Owen Gray admits it can be difficult to find a co-star willing to open up in the same way. He laments, "I wish that I had spent more time researching people's work who I considered doing content trade with and talked with them to understand their sexuality more before doing a scene with them." Broadway recommends researching MyFreeOnes.com and checking out their Clips4Sale website or prior scenes, to get a sense of what kind of performance they can provide.

Alt porn star Bella Vendetta champions the notion that small investments spent on the opportunity to work with great artists will pay off down the road. "Paying for one *excellent* shoot that will get you noticed can lead to so much other work."

2. *Get on the same page.* "Always make sure you know all of the details for a content share or trade, before you arrive to set. Don't leave anything un-discussed, because you don't want to find yourself in the midst of a miscommunication while on set." Siri lays it out, offering helpful considerations: "If you're not shooting at your own home or the other performers' home, make sure you understand the location arrangement – whether the location owner is letting you use their space for free, for a fee that the performers will split, or for a traded scene. And clarify beforehand, who is shooting the scene. Will there be one camera or two? Are you bringing your own videographer? Is another performer bringing a videographer, and if so how is that person going to be paid? Will there be a still photographer on set and is that person being paid, and how? Who is editing the scene, and are you going home with the raw footage?" Don't be shy to ask questions and talk it through.

3. *Paperwork and IDs.* Whenever possible, get your paperwork and ID photos squared away ahead of time. "Nothing takes away the sexy like many pages of paperwork and ID photos," says Mod. While it may not be sexy, it's a necessity. "Don't neglect your record-keeping," warns Shakti. "It'll bite you in the ass."

   Shares and trades still must obey the law. "I would recommend using the same model release and treat everything the same as a standard scene," says Deen. He also recommends contacting an attorney to finalize the forms, which detail exclusive content licenses.

Siri reminds us "that under 2257 law, anyone you share or trade content with has the right to sell that content to a third party, thereby disclosing your legal name and IDs. I like to add a clause to my release stating that the content may not be sold to a third party, or any of my personal information disclosed, without my prior written approval; and I also verbally confirm that with whomever I'm sharing content."

4. *Deliverables.* Decide when and how you will get your content. If you're taking home raw footage, bring equipment (memory cards, laptop, external hard drive) with you to store the files. Make sure your media requirement is compatible!

   Broadway advises those who outsource the technical aspects of production: "Don't be afraid to have your editor or webmaster get involved in the discussion. I would much rather answer questions before the shoot than have to reformat and resend content because what was asked for was not what was really needed."

   Being clear about the footage is important, as everyone has a different process. "We actually had a girl refuse to do trade with us because she couldn't walk away from the shoot with her footage (we shoot most scenes with three broadcast standard cameras, and the raw footage runs a gigabyte a minute per camera, so we usually have raw footage ready the next day). We thought that it was funny that she would refuse content that's of a higher quality that she normally gets, but understood that she had probably been burned by missed promises in the past." Whether the files can be taken home that day, or a future date is agreed, make arrangements ahead of time.

   Depending on the setup, you may simply choose to bring your own camera. "If you'll be shooting on tripod with no videographer, try to have each model's own video camera on two tripods, side-by-side," advises bondage producer Lorelei Mission. "This way you'll have your footage to take home right away, instead of having to rely on anyone else to make copies for you."

5. *A Satisfying Release.* Especially with shares, it's best to set a general timeline for releasing the content. "I try to make sure we're releasing our shared content within a week or two of each other, or at most a month – that way one of us isn't getting too much of a 'head start' on sales of the shared content," says Siri.

   Darling notes that two separate shoots can also eliminate the issue around releasing identical, shared content. With completely different shoots, they can be released as desired.

All of these should be considered and discussed before picking up the camera or stepping foot on set.

TROUBLESHOOTING

- *Missed Connections.* Lorelei addressed the issue of working with performers in terms of location and timing. "If your peer keeps canceling and rescheduling, schedule the next one to be where they live. Some performers are simply more likely to go through with a shoot if they don't have to drive anywhere. If your peer keeps canceling and rescheduling, evaluate the start-times you've been requesting. Instead of a morning start, try an after-lunch start time. If even that doesn't work, try a mid-afternoon start time, with a pizza break for dinner and then resuming shooting in the evening."

Without the incentive of a paycheck, and even among friends, planning a shoot can mean going the extra mile. "Be *extra* organized and on top of the shoot – often times if people aren't getting paid, they're more apt to cancel at the last minute, be late, be unresponsive (communication-wise), and just generally not take it as seriously," advises Shakti. "Constantly check in with your crew, and it will set you up for success."

- *Film Screenings and Promotion.* Ms. Naughty says doing content shares for BrightDesire.com with Zahra Stardust and Pandora Blake was a learning curve. She brings up issues that may arise for the film's future when working with colleagues, such as whether the footage can be used as promotional materials for affiliates and trailers. With erotic films, there are issues regarding who is in charge of festival submissions and premieres.

  Plan to discuss promotion all the way down to the watermark. "You'll always want to watermark your content with your logo," says Vendetta. "When you are shooting for content trade it's really common to have two different watermarks on images or video. But make sure you talk about this first!"

BONUS: GOING GLOBAL?

It's a small world, with growing number of collaborative opportunities for performers and producers overseas. Being literally on new terrain, it is now imperative that you know your laws. Start by asking the locals. "It's helpful to talk to other producers to learn about the legalities of porn production and distribution, especially with working with people from other countries," shares Gray. Remember that when shooting in the United States, US government-issued IDs are required for 2257 forms. When filming abroad, the laws surrounding pornography will depend on the country.

TO SHARE OR TRADE?

Trades tend to work best if both parties have similar levels of distribution, or, says Broadway, "if they each have different but specific needs, like one needs an adult baby scene and the other needs a forced orgasm scene."

"Consider doing two separate shoots to focus on what each performer wants rather than trying to fit everything in to one if the ideas don't work naturally from the beginning," says Gray. "Sharing a scene with the other performer(s) in that scene never dilutes my own sales, as far as I've been able to observe," notices Siri. "Part of that is because when I do content share, I generally do it with other performers whose markets don't overlap too much with my own. And when there is market overlap, like when I share content with another naturally busty performer, even then my sales stay the same. I like to keep the 'pool' of content sharers as small as possible, ideally so that only me and the other performer(s) on camera own rights to the scene."

POSITIVE OUTCOMES

Expanding a brand is also an opportunity for growth within the industry. A number of performers highlight the positive outcomes of working with trades and shares.

For some, it's a chance to get familiar with the inner workings of the genre and get in touch with their passions for the industry. "My curiosity in learning how to film, edit, do paperwork, and hopefully put out something positive into the world of porn is mostly what fueled making content for me," says Gray.

Kane highlights an often-overlooked incentive to be gained from content shares and trades: cross-promotion. "There is also value in shooting content with established performers from a social media aspect. You two can Tweet and cross-promote each other to generate more sales for yourself, and also gain new followers."

Queer porn director Tobi Hill-Meyer points out that doing trades can help increase performing opportunities. "Doing trades allows me to do what I love more often and get my face out there." And Vendetta reminds us that content trades and shares can propel a career. "I always tell people to make a dream list of people they'd like to work with. And work your way up the list. You can do it if you bust your ass!" By building a portfolio, you'll also be establishing relationships with other models, performers, and producers.

I wish I'd had all this advice two years ago. Though now I'm better suited for the next opportunity to come. Never again will I so obliviously forgo paperwork, and take such a risk on my best performances – I love what I do and want my videos to see the light of day! I've learned that for the right performer, someone dedicated and organized, the act of collaborating with other industry professionals in either trades, shares, or barter for services can create unique content that has the potential to elevate careers, provide income, and birth new production studios with new, inspired filmmakers. With careful planning and clear organization, trades can be a win-win. (Or if you prefer: a win for you, and then a win for me.)

7 LET'S BUILD A WORLD!

◆

WHEN YOU ARE WRITING A SCRIPT, YOU'RE BUILDING A world. What will that world look like? Who will the characters be? How will those characters explore and express their sexuality on film? What is the backdrop for this world? What are the major conflicts or challenges that your characters face? What tensions exist? What motivates your characters? These are all questions to ask yourself as you are brainstorming the script concept for your film.

Before you write a shot list or a script, you need to have a concept. For me, these concepts bloom from different things – sometimes from a dream I had, or from a theater piece, work of art or poem that inspired me.

My film *Art House Sluts* was inspired by the work of Andy Warhol and the creative movement that he cultivated at The Factory, including his work and collaborations with Edie Sedgwick. Some scenes in the film were directly inspired by, or even referenced, video art works and films by Andy Warhol, as well as feminist performance artists Yoko Ono and Carolee Schneeman.

My film *The Curse of Macbeth* was inspired by Shakespeare's theatrical play *Macbeth*. *Lesbian Life: Real Sex San Francisco* was inspired by the hit television series *Sex In the City*. *Writers and Rock Stars* was inspired by a poem that I wrote, titled "Writers and Rock Stars," about my real-life sexual experiences with musicians. *Perversions of Lesbian Lust* drew inspiration from the film *Tokyo Decadence*. *The StarrLust Experience* was largely inspired by David Bowie's Ziggy Stardust character. And my film *Tangled Heart Strings* drew inspiration from classic Russ Meyers films, David Lynch and Spinal Tap.

Sometimes my scripts and concepts are developed out of constrictions: of budget, or of access to certain locations or certain models. Sometimes I'm inspired by my community, my friends, fellow artists or political movements.

When I was directing my film *Sylvia*, which was inspired by the playwright AR Gurney's theatrical play of the same name, my concept was partially inspired by the theater piece, and partially influenced by my minimal budget and the knowledge that I needed to shoot the film in a single day.

This motorcycle garage served as a creative inspiration for this scene in *Fixed Gears, Fast Girls*.

I knew I needed to have a minimal cast with strong connections and compelling relationship dynamics. Talent is one of the biggest costs, and each day that you're in production, your location and crew budget is doubling, tripling or more. I also knew I wanted to create a film in which the film's narrative spans the course of a single day in a single location.

I recalled my experience as a teenager watching the play *Sylvia* at a small black box theater in Cincinnati, Ohio. The production features a couple, perhaps in their forties, who have just sent their child off to college. The woman in the couple finds the experience liberating. She can focus on her work and her life, and it's just the two of them. But the man in the relationship feels an emptiness and a want for more. When the man is out at the park he discovers Sylvia – a stray dog played by a human. The audience can hear Sylvia's inner dialogue and what she is attempting to communicate in dog speak.

The man is smitten with the pup and brings her home to meet Kate, his wife. Kate is not happy. She doesn't feel like they have time in their lives for a puppy. But the pup stays, and there is jealousy, tension, affection and love in this humorous love triangle between the puppy, the man and the woman.

I'll never know if my fellow theatergoers left that theater with the same erotic feelings that were conjured up for me that evening at the theater, but I'm not most folks. Looking back at that play years later when I was ready to write my next great opus, I realized what *Sylvia* was all about. It was totally a polyamorous, kinky-queer, puppy-play script, just waiting to be adapted for feminist porn. I adjusted the script accordingly, keeping some of the structure and dynamics from the play, but making it my own. Allow your own unique view of the world to come through in your shots, in your story, and you will find that your voice as an artist and filmmaker strengthens with each film.

Other films of mine were inspired by what was happening in my life or in the lives of fellow performers. When three of my good friends in the queer, indie, erotic film world became pregnant, I decided that we needed to create a documentary porn film about the desires of women during pregnancy.

In my searches I found a few films that were educational in nature around how to have sex when you're pregnant, but the majority of films featuring women during pregnancy appeared to be presenting it as a fetish – if at all. What I set out to create was a film that celebrated the individual woman, her transforming body, and the way in which she chose to express her sexual desire and pleasure at different points during her pregnancy: something that had yet to be done at that point. The resulting film was *Pregnant with Desire* – a docu-porn film.

Sometimes the concept for a film derives from the performers themselves. I worked with one couple for about six months on their scene for *Women Reclaiming Sex on Film.* It took one day to shoot, but finding the right partner and right location, and getting all the details in place, took months. Once we were in production, the greatest challenge was keeping my eight months' pregnant belly out of the frame. It's really empowering and exciting to open up the project to performers and collaborate with them in creating a script that specifically caters to their fantasies. When I operate in this manner I bring in the performers to develop the concept, and then I break down the concept into specific shots and dialogue.

Before you begin writing a shot list, let's try to define what a shot is. When you're watching a film, you are watching a string of moving photographs assembled one after the other to tell a story. Below you will find a series of shots from the shot list I composed for my film *The StarrLust Experience.* I've also included what the resulting shots looked like when we shot them on set.

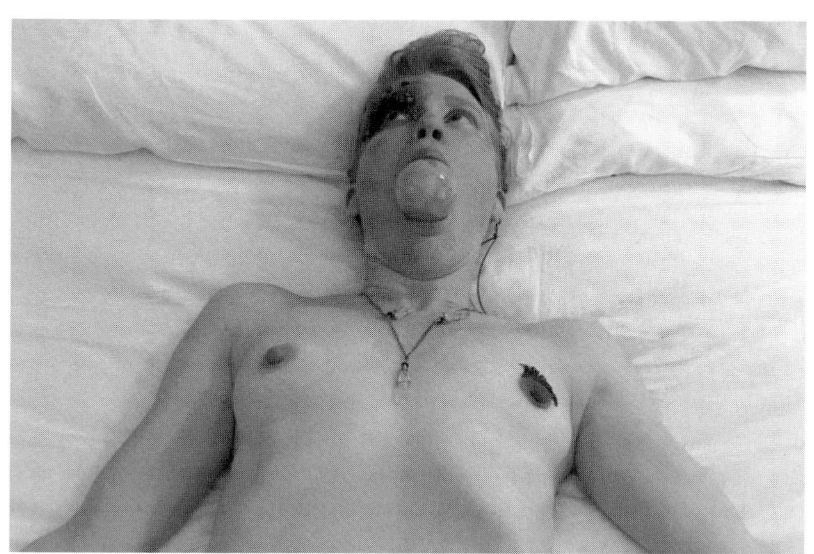

Shot of Mowie StarrLust lying down on the bed staring at the ceiling

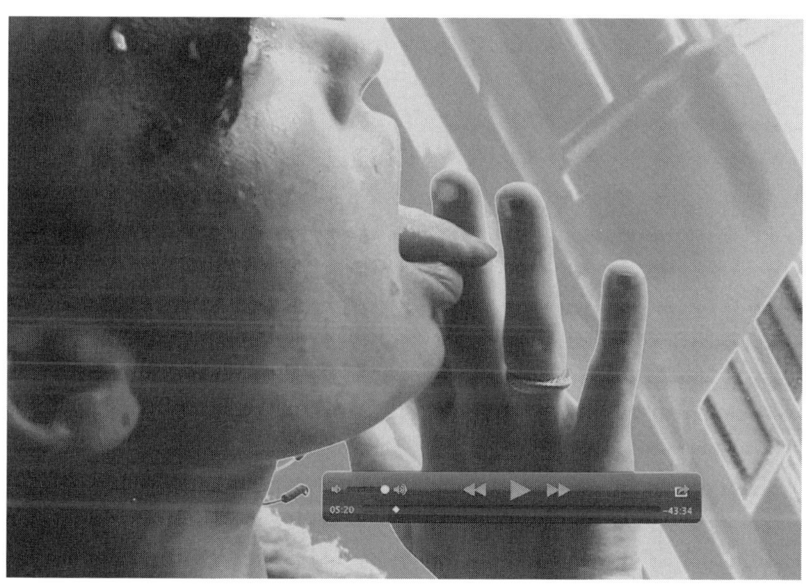

Shot of Mowie looking out the window

Shot of Mowie bouncing on the bed

Shot of Mowie making faces in the mirror – "Kept up here like a dancing monkey. Fuck it all. Where's the party when the cameras have gone home? No one here now, is there?"

MONOLOGUE – WRITING COMPELLING MONOLOGUE FOR A SINGLE PERFORMER

You don't need multiple performers in order to have compelling relationship dynamics and compelling monologues in your script. Below I've shared with you a small excerpt from my script *The StarrLust Experience.* The monologue is pulled from a scene in which the main character, Mowie, is talking to her reflection in the mirror and having a conversation with her body parts, giving voices, movement, and an identity to her Cunt, Anus and Tits. What results is a humorous and compelling single-person dialogue (dialogue = multiple characters, monologue = one performer) that bring us into the fractured ego and existential identity of the character's relationship with herself and her body.

(Mowie starts talking to her body parts – still staring into the mirror.)

Mowie: Hello, Cunt. You haven't left me, have you?

Cunt: (Mowie still speaking): Hello there. No I'm right here, Mowie. Want to play? Want to party.

Mowie: And you're here, tits, aren't you?

Tits: (still Mowie): Why yes, we haven't left you, Mowie!

Mowie: Very good. Very good. Perhaps we shall party, just the four of us.

Anus: (Close shot of Mowie puppeteering her anus by pulling at her butt cheeks): Don't forget about me!

Mowie: Who was that?

Anus: (Long shot of Mowie still puppeteering her anus) It was me, Anus. Don't forget about me.

Mowie: Oh no, we mustn't forget about Anus. No no no. That won't happen. We love you too much. Don't we?

(Action/Sound: Knock at the door)

Mowie: (Startled) Oh, fuck! Who is that?

Tits (Mowie jiggling them): Anus.

Mowie (Speaking to her tits and anus): No! No! That's not anus. Anus is right here. Who's at the door? Now quiet back there.

Mowie: (Speaking to her reflection in the mirror) Pull yourself together, Mowie.

(Action: Mowie opens the door)

DIALOGUE – WRITING COMPELLING DIALOGUE FOR MORE THAN ONE PERFORMER

Writing dialogue for DIY porn can be challenging; it's tricky to know how much dialogue to write, and how to develop the characters through the words that they are speaking. When I am writing a narrative that is somewhat dialogue-heavy, like the dialogue I've included below from my art house DIY porn film, *Tangled Heart Strings,* I make sure the performers have time to study the script, and let them know they can make the dialogue their own. If they change a couple of words and tell the story in a way that is most natural for them, I'm completely happy with that. I also keep one production assistant "on book," meaning that one person is holding the script off screen, and if a performer pauses for a couple of beats or calls out, "line," then the production assistant calls in the next line. Often I can shoot dialogue one line at a time if I need to. Just remember to change your shot between cuts.

When I was in the editing process for this film, I realized that some of the dialogue felt redundant and felt as if it was dragging on too long, so I ended up not using it all. However, having so much coverage of the dialogue really allowed me to pick and choose what I wanted to use to sculpt the edit.

In the dialogue below we see a discussion between the characters H (who is a queer rock star in love with their guitar), Siouxsie (a femme lover of H who is experiencing feelings of jealousy toward H's guitar), and Goddess Arboreal (a sex and relationship coach who is consulting the couple on the topic of polyamory and jealousy).

Goddess Arboreal: Inhale with me. Inhale the juicy, sexy, dripping wet orgasmic energy in the air and exhale any inhibitions, any judgments. This is a safe space for your emotions to run free like wild ponies. Let your ponies run, my loves. Let your ponies run. H, would you like to go first?

(Silence)

Goddess: Siouxsie?

Siouxsie: Um, well... We've been having some complications

Goddess: Hmmm... Yes.

Siouxsie: And, well, I feel like I've been replaced. I feel like I'm being pushed away by the person I love.

Goddess: That's it, Siouxsie. Let your ponies run free.

Siouxsie: I don't mind sharing a lover, but I feel... well, alone and hurt when all their attention is on Ibanez and, well, not on me. It hurts, Goddess Arboreal, and I just want my sexy rock star back in my arms. I want to feel that rush, that passion, that connection again. Do you think you can help us?

Goddess: Good, Siouxsie, good. Now turn to H and tell them how you feel.

Siouxsie: When you don't listen to me it hurts. I feel disconnected from you and I want you back in my arms. I feel like I'm losing you.

H: How can you say that? Every moment that I'm not on tour, that I'm not on that stage, baby, I'm with you.

Siouxsie: You're not just with me. You're with her. She's always there and she always has your attention.

H: I love you both.... You knew about Ibanez before we started dating.

Siouxsie: But I want things to change. I don't feel like there is room for me in your life when she is there.

Goddess: This is good. We are uncovering the pain. Our beauty lies in our vulnerability. Our pleasure lies beneath our pain. H, when did you last feel connected with Siouxsie in an intimate or romantic way?

DIY PORN ASSIGNMENT

What I'd like for you to do is turn on a film right now. This can be either an erotic or non-erotic film. Watch the film and try to identify the specific shots, the individual photos that the videographer has taken and how they are being assembled. Pay attention to the pace of the cuts, and how those choices of shots, either successfully or unsuccessfully, are telling you a story, informing you about the characters, evoking a certain emotion. Record your observations in your filmmaker's journal.

SKETCH OUT YOUR CONCEPT

What is the concept of your film? If you are creating a full-length feature film, organize that concept into four sex scenes. If you are filming a short film for screening purposes, you might only have a single sex scene.

If you choose to, you can then add small scenes between those four sex scenes, to act as narrative transitions that inform the viewer about the characters, relationships or performers.

If you were going to break down one of these concepts and each of these scenes into a string of shots, what would that look like?

Lie down and gently close your eyes, visualizing your shooting location, characters, and the concept of your first scene. It's time to watch your film for the first time, to develop those clear images of what your film will look like through the viewfinder. This is your initial creative rough draft, playing frame by frame in your mind. Allow the credits to start to roll: what do you see? Your initial idea can be your anchor, the core of your creative work, but also allow yourself to stray from that draft and be open to the imagery and surprises that enter your set.

On the set of my most recent film, *Tangled Heart Strings,* I was shooting my performers in a romantic comedy montage. The montage was actually the first visual that came to me regarding this film.

The concept of the film was based on three individuals in a polyamorous triad relationship: one genderqueer rock star, one hot femme, and the third, the rocker's guitar. The comedic and erotic nature of the film is rooted in the humorous relationship between

I grabbed this B-roll footage guerilla-style, out at Pier 39 in San Francisco.

a musician and their guitar. In a montage flashback, the rocker is neglecting their femme partner and having a big make-out fest with their guitar, and you can see the jealousy building on the partner's face and in her body language. I went to Pier 39 in San Francisco with the cast and crew to shoot the montage, including cliché romantic shots of the three individuals lapping ice cream, gazing out at the Bay and the Golden Gate Bridge, riding a carousel. And then a totally magical and unscripted moment presented itself.

One of our previous production assistants had taken a job as a pedicab driver at the Pier, and appeared out of nowhere. Why not get footage of the performers on the pedicab? It was perfect, and our old production assistant was happy to be of assistance and to make a cameo in the film, providing all of our feminist porn pedicab transportation needs. The point being, visualize your masterpiece and then set it free. Let it dance and be open to transformation and change. See where it leads you. Try not to control the film. but guide it instead, and facilitate the space and tools it needs to breathe, grow and manifest. If you have a cast already for this film, allow those characters to appear and play, see what they do in the locations that you had in mind. Allow the stories of your film to unfold. Your performers do need communication surrounding vision and expectations, but they don't need for you to over-direct every detail.

As your story is unfolding, also be mindful of how you are viewing the story. What images are stringing together in your mind to create these stories? Close-up shots of a woman exiting through subway doors, shots from across bustling traffic of a woman crossing the street? Where do your eyes, gaze and lens focus as you are visualizing your film?

This is one of many ways to start the process of writing your shot list. You won't be perfect at it in the beginning. You are learning by doing. The more you do, the more you exercise these muscles of constructing shots, and curating and assembling your shots together, the stronger those muscles will get, and the easier it will become.

When you have finished your visualization exercise, get out some index cards and write down one shot per card. Lay out the cards in the order in which they appeared to you. Now you can also play around with the order of your shots and think about how the assemblage of them will take the viewer on a different journey, how viewers will perceive the story slightly differently or experience a different emotional reaction, based on the order in which they view the shots.

When you have had plenty of time to play with the order of your shots, compile them into a single document and share this shot list with your videographer. You want to make sure that you and

Rigging a camera to a pedicab for *Tangled Heart Strings.*

your videographer are clear and on the same page before production starts. Sometimes when we write our shot list it seems very clear to us, but someone might read your shot list and have a very different vision from yours. Clear communication, compassion and patience as you learn one another's styles, is key to developing a strong team and articulating your vision. If you work with a single videographer numerous times, you will become more skilled at learning how to support the vision of a film project together. Your shot list will also be key for your editor, if you're bringing someone in to edit, or for you to refer back to if you are the one editing.

WRITER'S BLOCK

Are you coming up empty-handed when it comes to story or narrative that you want to shoot? You have a solid Vision and Values for your filmmaking practice, and you have even gathered a stellar team to collaborate with, including performers, but you're having no luck with creating a specific narrative.

Revisit your models' profiles and information from your interviews with your performers for inspiration. You want this film not only to represent your vision, but to support the sexual expression of your performers. Allow your performers' ideas, fantasies and experiences to guide the creation and inspire the narrative and scene.

For my film *Femmetastic,* Dylan Ryan and I shot this renegade-style solo scene in a laundromat and had a lookout positioned outside the door while I shot the footage.

Along with the performers' profiles that address their desires and fantasies, be mindful of their limits and comfort, as well as available locations that you might have to shoot in.

At a loss for a story, but your best friend owns a flower shop and totally loves that you are about to shoot DIY porn? Allow your story to blossom in this fortuitous setting. Do you know someone with access to a café? Do you live in a cool warehouse with a beautiful roof deck? Does your partner work at a motorcycle shop? What locations might you have potential access to, and do any of these locations hold inspiration for you when paired with your performers' fantasies? Sex and desire are everywhere, so exhale – let go of any previous concepts that might be creating blocks, and let your imagination run wild.

When writing a scene for your performers, you want to spend some quality time communicating with them to make sure that it is a scene with roles that resonate for them, that gives them choice surrounding how they choose to express their sexuality. It's important to pair performers up with a role and scene where they will blossom, open up and feel natural and celebrated for who they are.

When I'm communicating with a model prior to writing the script, the typical email that I send out to performers I've already cast and have met with in person looks like this:

"In constructing the scenes for my films, I like to make sure there is a lot of communication prior to the production to facilitate the most pleasurable experience for all of our performers. Things we may want to discuss include your turn-ons, fantasies, limits and turn offs, what gets you hot, whether you like toys, hands, mouths, boundaries and anything else about how you visualize this scene.

"Most importantly, I'm here to help facilitate an incredibly hot sexual experience for you. I'm very honored to have the opportunity to document these intimate moments on camera along with my

crew. Think of me as your sexy fairy godmother. Anything that can make this experience better for you, let me know. If you need a bowl of green M&Ms in order to feel sexy, I'll get the green M&Ms. If you feel really sexy fucking in heels, or you have a favorite pair of sneakers or cowboy boots that give you a hard-on, then you should totally wear them. I'm a big fan of communication, so let's start talking about your fantasies and I'll work on making them a reality."

Searching for more ways to break writer's block? Set your timer for five minutes and create as many one- to two-line pitches for films as you can. Try not to let your pen stop and just keep writing. Try this in your filmmaker's journal. No one needs to read it and the ideas don't even need to be further developed; just try to avoid judgment, critique or over-thinking. Just write in a stream of consciousness – short, one-line pitches and potential titles that are influenced by the vision and values that you have previously outlined. Pitches might look something like this:

1. LOVE, LUST, & SEX: REAL COUPLES; REAL CHEMISTRY

Series of videos that feature real couples, interviewing them about their relationships and featuring sex that is filled with the type of intimacy and beauty that you find amongst couples.

2. NEW EXPERIENCES

A series of films that features women and men's first experiences in front of a camera and walking them through that process. This series would be just as focused around the emotional journey, and empowerment of the performers' experiences and the choices and control that they have over creating the environment and fantasy, as the actual scene itself.

3. SIN-A-HOLIC

Do you have a craving for something sweet? At this vegan bakery, hot sex and illicit affairs are served up with sticky sex and tasty hot buns.

Looking for more ways to develop your ability to write scripts and shots for your film?

Try playing "I Spy" when you are watching films. This can boost your DIY pornographer muscles. When you are watching a film, what shots do you spy? What part of the person's body is in frame? How close or far away is the shot? Is the character walking into the shot, or what is the camera focused on? What does that particular shot tell us about the narrative? How do you feel and what emotions are you experiencing as you look at this shot? Pause the movie you're watching throughout, and really focus on the shots, one at a time. Identifying how films are made and focusing on the shots in other films will be helpful in honing the shots in your own filmmaking.

Practice, practice, practice. You don't have to shoot an entire film to practice assembling shots. Use yourself, your friends or your partners as guinea pigs in your filmmaking. You don't even have to take your clothes off. Just practice how to tell a story with pictures.

You can practice this by using a still camera, video camera or just your smart phone. Once you have assembled the images, try experimenting with how the shots feel when set to different musical soundtracks, when you slow the images down, when you assemble them in a different order. Experiment with the rhythm and repetition of the shots.

For example, try the practice shots that I've listed below, just taking photographs. Try capturing the shots again using a video camera. Play around with depth, angles and how close you are to your subject. Afterward, you can assemble the images in an iMovie or iPhoto slide show, and make your little flip book of shots that tell a story.

Shot of bathtub faucet spout dripping (long shot)

Shot of bathtub faucet spout dripping (close up)

Shot of person's bare feet on tile floor

Shot of hand on the bathtub nozzle, turning the nozzle

Long shot of bathtub and water running – person stands facing tub, back to camera

Shot of person's feet stepping into water in the tub, wearing clothes

Shot of water rushing from the spout into the tub

Close shot of water that is gushing from the spout coming in contact with the water already in the tub

Shot of feet further under water

Shot from within the tub of the person looking directly into and past the camera with a blank expression (medium shot)

Shot close on person's face looking past the camera with blank expression

Close shot of person's eye

Close shot of both eyes

Close shot of nose

Close shot of mouth (still blank and emotionless)

Close shot of mouth (a smile starts in the corner of the mouth) – we stay tight on the mouth shot while the subject struggles to smile

Close on mouth as the person exhales into a smile

Close shot of hands under the water

Close shot on hand turning off the water with nozzle

Close on faucet spout dripping

Want to try experimenting with slightly more sexual shots? Try the above shot list but try it with the person – the subject of the shots – naked in the tub. You can also add a close shot of a hand reaching for and touching their breast, thigh, cunt, penis or grabbing their own hair. Experiment with this list of shots and see what manifests.

The point of the shot list is so the videographer knows what to shoot and the editor knows in what order to assemble or curate the images back-to-back – and remember, that might be you.

My recommendation is that you get some practice in every role of production and post-production. Even if you don't have much interest in shooting video or editing and you are only really inspired by directing, learning how to shoot video and do basic editing and basic DIY lighting will all be incredibly helpful in your creative process, as a director and in your communication with any crew that you are collaborating with.

In proper DIY fashion, I often combine my script and shot list. However, the script typically contains things like where the performer moves, direction for the performers regarding action, the performer's dialogue, and the emotion in which they might be delivering the lines. The shot list is the visual, the pictures that the videographer is capturing. Experiment with both documents and see what format for your shots and performer directives work best for you in your DIY porn making.

8 GATHERING RESOURCES & CREATING A DIY PORN BUDGET

LET'S DELVE INTO A DIFFICULT TOPIC FOR MANY ARTISTS: *money* and *budget*. As an artist and maker within the DIY movement, I value creation and process over budget and profit. My goal and vision is to make a film, not a profit. However, to continue to create my art, my films and my writings, I have had to consider the expense, time and energy involved in manifesting a project, and how to sustain myself and my family through the creation of my art.

What helped me develop a healthier relationship with budgets and finances was learning to think of a budget as a communication tool that outlines the needs, expectations, desires and limits for a group of individuals, and signifies a mutual exchange of energy, goods and gratitude. Also, if you know that finances are not really your forte – not a language that you speak very easily – remember to reach out to others who are more proficient in finance, either to consult with or to partner with when you need help. This is part of building your team – finding allies and folks to collaborate with, who bring an assortment of different strengths to the table.

The actual moving parts of a budget can vary greatly. I have created films that were entirely based on trading skills, content and services in exchange for the production elements, and only paid for editing, post-production replication, printing and design of the box cover. In this way I have been able to keep costs for some films to around $2,000. If I hadn't intended to distribute those particular DVDs, I could have cut that cost as well.

In ten years' time, I have directed films with budgets as small as $2000-$4000 (*Undone, Writers and Rock Stars, Lights Out, Perversions of Lesbian Lust, Sylvia*), and films with budgets of close to $20,000 *(Fast Girls Fixed Gears).* Quite honestly, my lower-budget films have tended to be some of the most award-worthy, have garnered the most attention at film festivals, and have sold the best. A $10,000 budget allows for me to comfortably pay everyone industry rates without expending a lot of energy in trading, bartering and soliciting donations of services or supplies. When you first start out, you will probably have more energy than money to put behind a project, so scraping together resources is essential to the DIY porn budget.

When I direct films with bigger budgets for companies other than my own, the producers tend to want to have more control over the film. The more the producer interferes with the creative process of a filmmaker, the more difficult it is for the director's vision to be realized, and the more distorted the original vision of the filmmaker becomes. If you decide to work with a producer, or to direct or pitch a film project to another company, make sure there is a clear agreement between you and the producer that you feel good about. Define your needs and desires as a director, your creative boundaries; if you don't state these up front in writing, you risk really losing your vision in what becomes someone else's project.

The most successful experiences I've had working with a producer was for the films that I directed for Good Vibrations' film companies, Heart Core Films and Reel Queer Films. Good Vibrations' ethics and values aligned with my vision as a filmmaker. The company listened to and supported my creative pitches, and allowed me full creative control of my scenes, casting, narratives, soundtrack and editing. They proofed the films, and if there were notes on things that the company needed changed, they would send the notes my way and I'd work with my editor to meet the desires of the company. Their in-house graphic designer worked with me on the creative concept and text for the box covers; we were able to honor one another's creative vision and avoid any mistakes or miscommunications through thorough, creative conversations. We were a team and it was a good fit.

If you are not clear on what elements of the film will be under your creative control, you can run into problems and miscommunications surrounding the vision for the project. It's very important to develop a team that communicates clearly and understands the vision for your film from beginning to end. I've started off with a really great concept, and even had companies give me a fair amount of control on the production floor, but then they've ruined the film in post-production by taking over, not following the shot list, and just throwing together audio. Also, they didn't give me, the director, an opportunity to proof the film, which ruined the story.

If, as a photographer, you shoot a roll of photos, you know there are some beautiful photos on that roll of film, but only three or four that are suitable for exhibition. If you hand over that roll of film to some guy who didn't just pour his heart and soul into the film, he's going to print your blurry test shots from when you were testing the exposure; he will print those photos on cheap printer paper at Kinkos, and staple them to the wall or secure them with thumb tacks. It's telling some kind of story, but not the one you as photographer necessarily meant to tell. Fractured Communication + Non-Cohesive Vision = Fractured End Project.

It's easy when you are a new and eager director to sign the first contract that you're presented with, or to jump at the opportunity to direct for a company that is willing to produce your project. Celebrate the offer, take a deep breath and stick to the creative limits, needs and desires that you have as a director, to support the execution of your vision. This clear negotiation prior to production will make for a smoother, healthier experience with your producer and any outside production companies you might be working with.

My personal preference is to direct my own films, own the film outright and retain full control from concept to distribution. It's a lot more work, but the final project is a great payoff, and when you own your film you will be making money off of it for years.

As a filmmaker, I put more hours into the film than anyone else, and I do care. So do it yourself. Either fundraise $20,000 and pay your performers and crew super well, or do it for $2,000 and work your ass off, trading on any and every skill you have.

You might be saying, "Madison, what skill could I possibly have that is awesome enough to pay for my film?" Well if you're a performer, you're set. As you may have guessed, the performers are the most valuable element of a film. You might be saying, "Isn't the filmmaker or person holding the camera the most valuable player?" Nope. You can have a completely static camera on a tripod, or have the performers themselves holding the camera, and if you have a compelling performance captured on film, perhaps shaped into a simple but interesting narrative or concept, you're golden.

You can have the best videographer in the world, great lighting and an awesome location… and if you star is hung over, lacking in energy or simply not compelling, then the scene will suffer.

The most important thing with technical aspects of a film is that the audience not be distracted by them. Personally, I think this goes for both cinematography that is beautiful but distracting, or really shaky videography. Everything that happens should help tell your story. For example, you don't want the image to be so dark that you can't follow the performers or the story. You don't want the audio to be so bad that you are distracted by the buzzing fridge instead of losing yourself in the moans of pleasure between the performers.

If the camera is shaking, I want it to be because the performer has grabbed the camera and is filming the action, because that is part of the narrative. If you are honest and true to the story and really hold space in supporting a stellar cast (even a cast of one), then you can create a great film.

A solid editor is probably my vote for the next most important person in your film production. You can also learn how to edit yourself. Sometimes I'll do the first edit and hand over my film to another editor to tidy it up a bit, add some pretty credits and smooth out any rough spots. Learning how to edit definitely helps improve one's abilities as a filmmaker and director. If you don't edit yourself, make sure to work closely with your editor for the reasons I mentioned earlier in this chapter.

An editor can really hack your film and make you look horrible, if not given proper guidance by the director. Make a film you love. Really love it. Fall in love with it every step of the way, because you will be watching it over and over and over again, along with the editor, bringing a critical eye to looking for props that shouldn't be there, or shadows, or reflections of the videographer in the glass of the grandfather clock that would totally ruin that shot of super-hot cunnilingus. You will be looking for the boom mic, and you will be watching your film again and again. So fall in love with it. Shoot what you love, what you're passionate about.

Each scene has a rhythm to it. You can tell when you're watching the film if the scene feels too long. If you start to feel bored watching a scene, make a note of exactly the moment in the film that this happens. If you feel bored and this is a film you love, then likely your viewer will be bored too. Your scene might need to be shorter.

Or you might need music. Some erotic filmmakers use music, some don't. My advice is to do what feels good to you and experiment. In many of my early films I incorporated music by local San Francisco bands. Many of them were totally excited about the idea of having their music in a film, and most donated their music in exchange for a credit at the end of the film. If you can pay the bands, pay them.

My most recent films, including *Tangled Heart Strings, Women Reclaiming Sex on Film, The StarrLust Experience*, my *Fluid* series, *Femmetastic* and *The Curse of Macbeth,* all have a composer scoring the film. The composer watches the films, or I'll describe the scene in detail, giving him the vibe, and he constructs simple, short songs that embody the appropriate emotions. If there are similar musicians who I feel embody the emotional experience I'm looking to convey in the music, then I reference those musicians as well, so I can give the composer further direction and so that we are in alignment with regard to musical tone and composition. I really enjoy music in my films, but I also like to hear sex, so I'm careful with where the music fits and where it doesn't, making sure not to cover up the characters' connection and pleasure, but moving along the energy of a film if it seems to be dragging.

So how, again, do you create a porn budget? Your budget will be unique to your film. You might just be creating an erotic short: single scene that is ten minutes in length. But if you're creating a full-length feature, there are traditionally at least four sex scenes, plus any narrative or interviews that support the story.

Often if I am on a tight budget, I try to shoot my entire film in a single twelve- to fifteen-hour day. It's exhausting. It truly is. As an example, here is the schedule and call sheet for my feminist porn-award-winning erotic film *50 Shades of Dylan Ryan*, which included a group sex party scene!

> Hi All,
>
> Below is a schedule, along with times and location for our upcoming shoot tomorrow. If you haven't yet connected with your scene partner, please do so. For wardrobe bring five or six different choices for outfits that you feel comfortable and sexy in. Below there are specifics on wardrobe as it pertains to each character and each scene.
>
> Try to avoid clothes that have busy designs and patterns, or logos. Please bring several undergarment selections as well. Nice lingerie, thigh-highs, heels, garters. Please bring any sex toys, dildos, vibrators, floggers, canes, ball gags, paddles that you enjoy, as

well as your favorite lube. If you have any preferences regarding food or any allergies, please let me know so we can accommodate.

We are running a very tight schedule, so please be on time or early for your scene. It will help us in moving smoothly from one scene to another. I'm really so thrilled to have such an amazing cast put together for this film. Please remember to bring your STI tests and US government-issued ID. If there is anything I can do to make your shoot more pleasurable, please do let me know.

Tomorrow we will be flipping the New York Times best-selling book *Fifty Shades of Grey* on its head in our script. I'm currently working on finalizing the script, but will send it as soon as it is finished.

with love and orgasms,
Madison

WARDROBE:

Sadie: Your character is an entrepreneur of a publishing company.

Scene 1 and 2 you are in "work" clothes - sexy, sophisticated, smart, dress slacks, button up shirts, sexy lingerie, heels. The "sexy boss." Pencil skirt or dress slacks, shirts where cleavage is showing, but professional looking.

Scene 3 and 4 you're in dominant fetish outfits - corsets, latex, leather, sexy, dominant, high class.

Please bring strap-on and dildos if you have them. Let me know if you have a collar you can bring for Dylan. Do you have rope or cuffs for bondage?

Dylan: Your character is a confident women's studies and literature major. She is femme, fearless, a little awkward and dorky, but self-assured and in her early/mid twenties. So maybe dress college chic for the brunch – simple dress with a cardigan. If you have glasses, that would be great.

The second scene you will dress similarly to the first.

Third scene, bring nice lingerie, thigh-highs, garters, heels. Same for the Fourth scene.

Berretta: nice lingerie, collar, heels, garter, thigh highs.

Bianca: Bring a couple of options for a nice Sunday brunch dress, sexy but sophisticated. Sexy lingerie, heels, garter, thigh-highs.

Scene 1: Brunch Scene: Sadie and Bianca (Sex/BDSM) Dylan (non-sex voyeur and dialogue)

Scene 2: Interview scene: Sadie and Dylan (Sex/BDSM scene)

Scene 3: Dylan and Beretta James (sex) while Sadie watches

Scene 4: Dylan Ryan fondling by extras and (Sadie/Dylan sexual BDSM interaction) (Bianca and Sadie interaction) (Dylan and Beretta interaction)

SCHEDULE:

Sept 3rd

Location PROVIDE PERFORMERS WITH ADDRESS AND ANY NEEDED DIRECTIONS

7 A.M. Set up

8 A.M.	Call time for Sadie, Bianca and Dylan
9 A.M.	Shoot set up shots – photos, and tease video
9:30 A.M.	Shoot sex and Scene 1
10:30 A.M.	Wrap Scene 1
11 A.M.	Shoot set up with Dylan and Sadie
12 P.M.	Shoot sex scene (Scene 2) w/ Sadie and Dylan
	Call time for Beretta
1 P.M.	Wrap sex Scene 2
1:30 P.M.	Set up tease video and photos for Beretta
2 P.M.	Sex scene 3 Beretta, Sadie (voyeur) and Dylan
3 P.M.	Wrap sex scene 3
3:30 P.M.	Shoot photos, teaser videos, any dialogue or b-roll that we are missing
4:30 P.M.	Extras call time
5 P.M.	Shoot Party scene
	(Sadie/Bianca)
	(Sadie/Dylan)
	(Dylan/Beretta)
	(Dylan/fondling from the extras)
7 P.M.	Wrap shoot

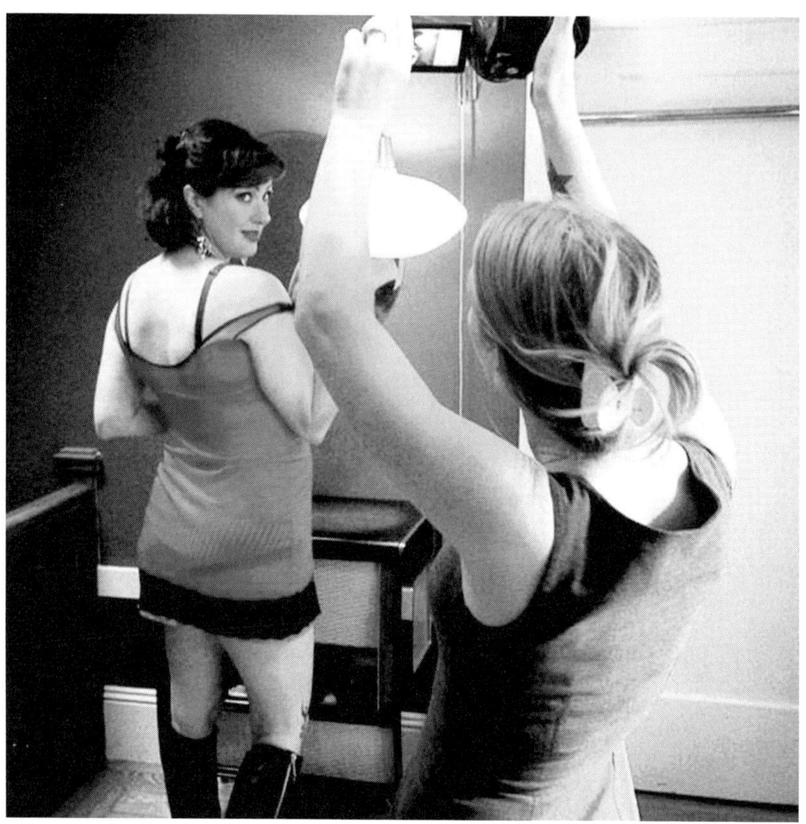

Shooting the sequel to *50 Shades of Dylan Ryan*, I wrote Sadie Lune's pregnancy into the plot line and had the honor of shooting her during her pregnancy.

As you can see, there is *a lot* packed into a day. While you might be feeling the pressure to keep everyone on time and on schedule, you also must be mindful to keep your calm zen-director-self present, and create a space for the performers that is stress-free and supportive.

Although this can be a lot to manage, a single day of shooting means only paying a day rate for your videographer, makeup artist, photographer and performers. If you are doing a single-day shoot, you are likely going to need to shoot at a single location, like a house with multiple rooms. Sometimes you can shoot two scenes in a single room if you change out some of the furniture, bring different bedding and wall art, or shoot from a completely different angle, depending on how big the room is.

When I'm lucky enough to have a more robust budget, I'll shoot in two days – two scenes on each day. This is luxurious, but it doubles your crew fees, location rate and food cost. Here are a few example budgets that I have worked with:

- **Performer:** $400 (per performer per scene). This really varies. A queer or girl /girl scene ranges anywhere from $400 to $700. For some of the bigger names, a g/g scene might even extend up to $1000. For a solo masturbation performance, the rate is anywhere from $200 to $500. A boy/girl scene is $900 to $1100. An anal boy /girl scene is $1100 to $1300 ($1200 is average). Remember, this is per performer.

  Let's assume you have four scenes with two people in each scene at $400 each, then your performer budget would be $3200. If you have fewer performers, or if you are also one of the performers, or if it is a film all about one compelling performer who is doing different solo masturbation scenes as she explores her sexual desires, then you can cut this number drastically.
- **Videographer/director of photography/cinematographer:** $400 to $800 per day, depending on the videographer. The level of skill needed here will vary depending on the project, but always interview and screen your videographers. Just because they are an ace at shooting basketball doesn't mean they will be comfortable and not lose their cool when they are shooting a sex scene. Examine their reel or projects they have shot, and if possible try to do a test shoot with them that is just a solo scene or something low-budget, so you can see how they shoot sex. Review the footage, give them notes, and let them know what they did that you like, as well as any modifications or things you would like them to keep in mind when they are shooting for your feature film.

You need to be very clear with your videographer regarding your shot list, lighting needs, and what you need to see and what you don't. Try not to get too frustrated. It's a learning curve for all of us, and as time goes on you will get clearer at articulating your vision.

Having adequate time in pre-production to speak with your videographer about the clear vision you have for your film can really pay off in the end result. If you aren't in front of the camera, it can be a great experience for you to operate the camera yourself, because you will know what shots you want. And if you don't get the shot, you have to be accountable for what you were able to capture, and learn how to articulate your shots and vision through practice.

- **Makeup artist:** Anywhere from $100 a day to $150 per performer for hair and makeup. The film that you are shooting and the makeup skills of your talent will determine whether you need a makeup or makeup and hair stylist. If your film is very natural, like really documentary style, then you might not need a makeup or hair stylist. If you do have funds I recommend bringing in a makeup artist for your features, but be picky about who does makeup and hair. Look at photographs and examples of their work and clearly communicate through both words and images the style of makeup you want for your performers.

  Also make sure that the character and style of hair and makeup you have envisioned is a style that resonates with your performer. If your performer is in hair, makeup and wardrobe that doesn't feel natural, sexy or comfortable, that will translate on film. Adapt the character's look to fit something that feels inspiring and exciting to your performers, and honors the way they wish to express their gender and sexuality.
- **Production Assistant/Photographer:** $50 to $200 per day. The PA is an important player in a DIY porn production. This person fulfills multiple roles and often also serves

Our makeup artist, Jolene Parton, helped us to achieve the gender-fluid Bowie-inspired rock star look we wanted for our film *The StarrLust Experience.*

as the photographer for a shoot. The PA might be taking both photographs for promotional use and behind-the-scenes photographs, setting up props, assisting with lighting. Additionally, the PA might be assisting with the needs of models, distributing water, lube or baby wipes, and acting as sort of a sex fairy during a scene. PAs might also be calling in lines for dialogue-heavy scenes. An awesome, on-task PA is invaluable.

Working as a PA can be a great way to learn how production works, and gives you the opportunity to learn different roles within production as well. Sometimes having two production assistants can be helpful, depending on the size of your location and whether or not you – the director – are performing or are behind the camera. If you as the director are taking on numerous roles, you might want an extra PA to assist with flow, production management and keeping the cast and crew on schedule.

- **Director: $1000 to $1500 per day.** If you have a budget for yourself as the director – which you should – the rate can span from $1000 to $1500. It can be more or less, depending on the company. As the director, you are going to spend countless hours crafting your film from its vision to the screening or distribution, so make sure to put a line item in for yourself. If you're working with a minimal budget, you can always pay yourself in post-production through sale of your film.

- **Food: $100-$150 per day.** Feed your performers and crew! These are long days, so you will either need to get take-out menus for local places that fit the dietary needs of your performers, or do a market run and have food bought for the day. Sometimes I hire a friend to cook for everyone, which can be a great way to make sure everyone is getting healthy, nourishing food. Also make sure there is a selection of snacks, coffee, tea and other drinks available throughout the shoot day. Fresh foods will not make your performers feel sluggish, but refreshed, cared for and nourished. Ask them what foods they like to eat and what their preferences and sensitivities to foods might be.

- **Props, Safer Sex Supplies and Wardrobe:** $100 to $200. This can vary and might all be stuff that is borrowed, along with safer sex supplies from a local free clinic. If the film is more stylized, you might need to purchase a few things for this line item.

- **Location: $50 to $400.** Sometimes you might be able to get a free location. I've used some incredible locations, like beautiful Napa vineyards which I shot at for films like *A Woman's POV Ciao Bella* and *A Woman's POV: Heartland*, which were donated to us for our shoots. Other spaces like warehouses, apartments, motorcycle shops and cafes I've rented for somewhere between $100 to $300, depending on the size, amount of time spent at the space, and how dependent we are on the location for our film. Other outdoor locations I've done completely renegade, like shooting in secluded areas of Golden Gate Park, the cliffs at Sutro Baths, and secluded areas of beach. This eliminates your location budget, but you still need at least one lookout, and a production assistant doing extensive scouting of outdoor locations prior to the shoot.

POST-PRODUCTION

- **Editing:** $500 to $800. If you decide to do the editing yourself on a feature film, you can avoid this expense. If you run into problem areas during your editing process, you can always call in an experienced editor to consult with, or to polish up your existing edit. Make sure to create a menu for your film, and PG-13 and explicit versions of a trailer for your film. Remember, if you are handing your film off for edit, communicate very closely with your editor and provide them with honest and productive feedback so that you are working together to manifest a single vision. Watching the edit together and giving feedback in conversation, or noting exact time markings where you found elements of the edit that did or didn't work for you, can be useful.

- **Music: $100 to $200.** If you decide to add music to your film, you can ask bands directly if they would be okay with you using their music in your film, credit them, and let them know how much you can compensate them. Find local bands

Wicked Grounds Cafe was a perfect location for this sexy queer scene between Dylan Ryan and Arabelle Raphael in *Fixed Gears Fast Girls*, and I was able to rent a location from folks in the LGBTQK community.

with a sound that resonates with your film and get them on board with your vision. Otherwise, finding a musician who can compose music for specific scenes has also worked out well for me. This is an excellent opportunity to expand your reach and to collaborate with artists in a different medium by working with musicians.

One mock budget that contains only production elements might look like this:

Budget for *50 Shades of Dylan Ryan*

Location: $400

Director/Videographer/ Photographer/Script writing $1000

Production Assistant $200

Talent: $4000 – 9 performers (including extras/4 sex performers, 4 scenes)

Props and Food (food, water, lube, baby wipes) $200

Total Budget: $5800

Or

Budget for *The StarrLust Experience*

Talent: $400 (one performer)

Videographer: $300

Makeup artist $150

Head PA/Stylist/Social Media/Photographer $150

Props $150

Food $100

Location $300

Director/Writer/Editor/2nd Performer $1000

Total Budget: $2500

◆

So what happens if you have no money to put toward your film? Should you just give up your dream? Absolutely not! When I first started my art gallery I didn't even have an apartment of my own, and I was living on food stamps. The term "starving artist" is real, and being a filmmaker and DIY pornographer is an art form. Don't give up your dream. If you make it, people will cum, and if you really believe in your vision it will manifest. The less money you have, the more you need to be really smart, resourceful, scrappy and prepared to work even harder.

I didn't have any money saved to make my first film, *Bondage Boob Tube*. But I did have friends who let me use their studio as a location in exchange for work as a model for some stock photography they were shooting. All of the performers I cast were close friends that also had their own websites, and I gave them the right to use the scenes they performed in for their own sites. My videographer was one of my only expenses. Sometimes it takes up to a year to shoot all the scenes of a film, so that you can pace out the budget and energy expended on the project. Experiment with different modalities, be open-minded and flexible, and look around you in your community and amongst your friends for what skills and resources you can bring together to manifest your vision. Keep making film and know that your vision and your film can not be stopped by lack of funds. There is always a creative way to make your own thing happen and to value everyone involved in your project.

One of the ways that you can bankroll a project is through fundraising efforts. Here are a few things to consider in raising funds for your film:

- **Crowdsource Funding.** Be careful with your wording and the platforms that you use to fundraise, as KickStarter and PayPal have both in the past confiscated funds and closed down fundraising campaigns that relate to pornography. I have had great experiences with Indieagogo and Patreon. Do some research on the online platforms' conditions, and what type of projects they support, so that you don't risk losing funds that you've worked hard to earn.

- **Live Fundraising Events.** This is a great way to let folks know about your casting, your company and your vision, while you raise funds. Consider screenings or dance parties where you screen porn clips from other DIY porn and feminist porn allies. Ask the filmmakers first. You will likely receive a resounding yes, as long as you credit the filmmaker. You can also reach out to local businesses and sex-positive toy companies and hold a raffle. Contact DIY and feminist porn stars and directors and hold an auction. By partnering with and publicly showing your alliance with other well-known feminist and DIY porn performers and directors, you give the public an idea of your values and politics, and what they might expect from you as a filmmaker.

- **Individual Funder or Silent Producer.** If you are really great at pitching your vision and your film before it is even shot, you can often find individuals who love your idea and would love to invest in your film

- **Pre-sale.** If you are able to shoot a trailer and have a strong vision for your film that you can sell to your audience, you can offer the public an opportunity to purchase pre-sale DVDs, pre-sale tickets to your premiere, or VIP experiences for theatergoers where they can meet the performers, etc.

SPECIFIC TAX INFORMATION FOR FILM PRODUCTION, BY THE TAX DOMME

The Tax Domme, www.taxdomme.com, is a tax preparer with a specialty in the Arts & Entertainment Industry, as well as a current member and advocate of the Adult Entertainment Industry.

CHOOSING YOUR BUSINESS STRUCTURE: SHOULD YOU INCORPORATE?

There are many reasons to incorporate and many reasons not to incorporate. The most popular reasons to incorporate are liability concerns, tax savings and raising capital. In film production there may be just one sole person creating a simple, short film, or there may be two or more people working together on a project. Therefore, it is vital that those responsible find a suitable business structure first, before investing in the film. This should be one of the first steps of film development as the film itself, especially if the film is made for profit and thus, a business of its own.

The first step to answering the two questions whether or not to incorporate and if so, which structure, is to know what the different types of business entities are. Each of these entities, after Sole Proprietorship, brings with them a certain degree of increased paperwork, fees and responsibility of the owner(s).

SOLE PROPRIETORSHIP

Description: A business owned and managed by one individual business owner and thus the simplest entity to have.

Liability: The business owner is personally liable for all debts and obligations of the business.

Tax consequences: Other than basic business operations, the business owner reports their income and deductions on their personal tax return. The result of their profit or loss is combined with the rest of the tax return and their Self Employment tax is figured in and paid along with their personal taxes.

Fees: There are no special fees associated with being a Sole Proprietor, only the Self Employment taxes associated with the business income. If the taxpayer chooses to use a tax professional, they only pay for preparation of their personal tax return and a state return if applicable.

Other responsibilities: There are no further responsibilities or obligations required of this type of business.

PARTNERSHIP

Description: A single business with shared ownership by two or more people. A Partnership can either be a General Partnership or LLC.

Liability: Partners share the full liability of the company's debts and obligations besides their own.

Tax consequences: The Partnership must file an annual information return, issuing Schedule K-1 to each partner. The Partnership does not pay taxes itself, but instead passes the income received to each partner, on which they pay the tax on their share of income on their individual income tax return.

Fees: If an LLC, the Partnership must furnish all applicable annual information returns, reports and fees to the state in which the LLC was created.

Other responsibilities: Partners must remember to properly allocate the proper percentage of income, dividends, expenses on the business account for personal use and changes in capital to each partner. Additionally, if there is a foreign partner, the Partnership is required to withhold 35% of the foreign partner's income for tax purposes. The Partnership is also required to file additional forms with their Partnership tax return and the foreign partner must acquire an Individual Taxpayer Identification Number that will require the foreign partner to file a US tax return with their ITIN application.

LIMITED LIABILITY COMPANY (LLC)

Description: A hybrid business entity that provides limited protection of a corporation but allows for the ease of being taxed as a Sole Proprietor or Partnership. Note that LLC stands for Limited Liability Company and not Corporation. The owner(s) of this business entity are called "members" and not "shareholders."

Liability: Members have limited liability in regard to the debts and obligations of the LLC.

Tax consequences: The income is reported on the member's 1040 tax return or other type of tax return depending on the type of LLC created. The income is then passed through to the member(s) via a Schedule K-1.

Fees: The LLC must furnish all applicable annual information returns, reports and fees to the state in which the LLC was created.

Other responsibilities: Annual state reports and tax returns are required.

CORPORATION

Description: A business entity that is completely separate from its shareholders. A corporation can be either a C-corporation that is a traditional corporation, or a Subchapter S-corporation.

Liability: Shareholders are most often not liable for corporate debts and obligations.

Tax consequences:

C-corporation. The corporation must furnish to the IRS and state, if applicable, all information returns. The corporation is taxed twice. First on the income it receives, and then the shareholders pay taxes again on their personal tax returns when dividends are paid out to them from the corporation. Some shareholders may also be considered employees, such as officers. These shareholders also pay taxes on their wages and must be furnished a W-2 at the end of the year.

Subchapter S-corporation. The corporation does not pay any income tax, but instead, the income passes through the corporation and to the owner, who pays the taxes on their income on their personal tax return. Some shareholders may also be considered employees, such as officers. These shareholders also pay taxes on their wages and must be furnished a W-2 at the end of the year.

Fees: The corporation must furnish all applicable annual information returns, reports and fees to the state in which the company was incorporated. In addition, there may be fees associated with the preparation and filing of payroll and payroll taxes.

Other responsibilities: Formal board and shareholder meetings and minutes are required, as well as annual state reports. Some shareholders, such as officers, are also considered employees and thus are required to receive their salaries on Form W-2 with other profit distribution on Schedule K-1.

PERSONAL LIABILITY LIMITATION

A common misconception is that incorporating your business will protect your company and you completely. This is not at all the case. Incorporation does separate you, the person from you, the company. However, there is very little stopping someone from suing you, the person, for the personal actions you perform separately from you, the company. Additionally, when applying for certain bank loans and leases you will be required to sign a personal guarantee, thus making you, the person, responsible for the debt incurred.

INCOME

It is important to know how you will pay yourself and others, and there are specific rules and regulations involved with each type of income.

EMPLOYEE VS INDEPENDENT CONTRACTOR

Generally under common law rules, someone should be considered your employee and receive a W-2 at the end of the year if you are able to control what will be done and how it will be done by the employee, even if the person working for your has been given freedom of action. This especially holds true if the employee is not allowed to work for anyone else except you. People who work for themselves and are in control over every aspect of their work, as well as the ability to perform work for more than one person, are considered self-employed Independent Contractors and receive from the payer a 1099-Misc at the end of the year. It is not possible to call someone who should be considered your employee an Independent Contractor simply because you do not want to perform payroll and file employment tax returns.

Some people do not fall under the common law rules and are called statutory employees. Some people that are statutory employees are:

- A full-time life insurance salesperson who sells for one company
- A person who works at home by the guidelines of the person for whom the work is done and the materials for work are provided to the employee and are then returned to the employer
- A sales person that travels and works full-time for only one firm

W-2

A W-2 form is what most people think of first when they think of taxable income. It's the form that your employer sends you at the end of January stating what you've earned in the past year, the total amount of tax that had been taken out of your check for federal and, if applicable, state purposes and is the most reported source of income. If your employer pays your social security and Medicare taxes and does not withhold those amounts from your pay, that amount is still considered wages and must be claimed along with your gross income.

You also must report amounts on other W-2s received from other jobs you held, as well as those of your spouse if applicable.

1099

This is income derived from work as an Independent Contractor for specific services rendered. This can be for ongoing services or as a one-time stint. Most often, taxes are not withheld, thus putting the tax obligation onto the independent contractor. However, one may request to have taxes withheld when working as such.

FILM PRODUCTION EXPENSES

Expenses beyond the general business expenses that are specific to film and web performers, directors and producers are:

- 2257 adherence costs
- Advertising expenses
- Agent fees
- Barrier removal
- Business Cards
- Camera & Video Equipment

- Casting agents (directors & producers)
- Catering expenses
- Cell phone (percentage for business)
- Choreography
- Condoms and lubricant
- Content (photo)
- Content (writing)
- Director of photography fee
- Education and training expenses including private tutors, workshops and conferences
- Film & processing
- Fixing in post fees
- Image capture and storage
- Legal fees including trademark and copyrights
- Location costs
- Makeup (cosmetics – makeup marketed as "stage makeup" only)
- Music (business-related percentage CDs, MP3s, etc.)
- Musical instruments
- Musicians, sound effect specialists and special effects specialists
- Professional editing
- Promotional expenses
- Props
- Rental/Lease (office, stage, room, equipment, storage, costumes, etc.)

- Repairs
- Scouting expenses
- Security guards
- Sound editing software
- Tickets to performances and concerts (used for research, inspiration and networking)
- Video editing software
- Videos and DVDs (for research and inspiration)
- Wardrobe (also alterations, cleaning, repairs)

"APPEARANCE & IMAGE" EXPENSES

Even though it is known that in the realm of Entertainment the costs of makeup and wardrobe are, in IRS terms, "ordinary and necessary" business expenses, the IRS has put specific limits in specific wording on what can be taken as a deduction.

First, please let me say that we tax professionals can only interpret the tax laws and follow them as we interpret them. However, when wording is specific, there is no magic power that we hold that can change it. We are not trying to be mean or difficult, but instead taking our clients' best interest into consideration. Knowingly taking non-allowed deductions is considered fraud, therefore a tax professional who cares for their clients at all will not lead them into these shark-infested waters.

Below are quoted excerpts from the IRS MSSP (Market Segment Specialization Program) - 1040 Tax Issues - Entertainment. This guide is what the IRS auditors are given to assess the entertainers who they are auditing. The guide is designed to provide assistance in auditing individuals in various aspects of the entertainment industry.

- *Make-up.* Make-up for performances is usually provided by the studio. Stage make-up that the taxpayer buys for an audition or a live theatrical performance may be deductible, if it is not a general over-the-counter product.
- *Wardrobe.* To deduct clothes as a business expense, two requirements must be met. First, the clothes must be required by the employer. Second, clothes must not be adaptable to street or general use.

  Expenses for costumes and "period" clothing are generally deductible. However, most union contracts provide for compensation to be given performers who require special wear. The taxpayer must prove that his or her contract did not include such reimbursement for the expense to be allowable.
- *Physical Fitness.* Deductions for general physical fitness are not allowable. Usually, if physical fitness is required of a specific job, the studio will provide the cost. If the taxpayer was employed in a capacity that required physical conditioning, allow expenses for the duration of employment if no reimbursement or compensation was available.

9 PRE-PRODUCTION: COMMUNICATION AND EMPOWERMENT

◆

FACILITATING SPACE FOR OUR PERFORMERS' AND crew's voices to be heard requires a building of trust through active listening, along with asking the right questions. I like to say "every individual is a sexual snowflake, all completely unique and different." Celebrating and honoring the expression of each individual is one of the key differences between commercially focused mainstream pornography and DIY feminist porn.

In your DIY porn-making endeavors, you will discover that some people find communicating about sex much easier than others do. Some people have never really been in a situation where they've been asked what their greatest sexual fantasy was – either on-screen or off. Reserving your judgments and providing a nurturing, positive space where folks can speak about their experiences and fantasies can be helpful in guiding and sculpting a scene with your performers.

Some people might feel like they know you already if they have seen you perform, speak publicly or read from your books. This may cause a couple of reactions: One, your performers feel super-comfortable because they feel like they already know and trust you. Or two, they feel really nervous, because they have built you up in their heads to be larger than life. In the end, we're all just human – trying to tell stories, trying to leave our own drawing on a cave wall in hopes that it helps others to feel a little less alone in this vast life.

If you are a brand-new director with no public persona, people will start to make their own perceptions about you as soon as you place a casting call, choose a name for your directorial work, and start blogging your ideas about the film you want to make. This is yet another reason why it is important to have a clear Vision and Values statement that you can keep coming back to, like your own North Star.

Above all, the way to build trust in relationships, with your friends, your crew and your performers, is by being honest and authentic about your vision and what you stand for, and to be open to hearing other points of view. In fact, you should encourage their points of view. In the same way that a dominant can learn a great deal about BDSM from listening to their submissive, a director can learn so very much by listening honestly and openly to their performers.

So what does this active listening look like? When a model contacts me and says they are interested in performing for one of my productions, I meet with them at a public place like a café. Ideally, you'll meet somewhere where your conversation can still have a sense of privacy. I've usually already corresponded online a couple of times to ask questions like "How old are you? What is your previous performance experience? What inspired you to apply as a performer for my production?" From these questions I will usually get a good idea regarding the performer's motivation to be a part of the production.

If the questions above lead to answers like, "I want to be a porn star because I need quick money, I want to be rich and famous, I'm trying to piss off my parents/boyfriend/girlfriend," or any similar motivations, I let the applicant know that I don't believe they would be a good fit for our production company at this time, and I wish them luck with their path.

Or I can I try to bring some reality to their situation, letting them know that porn is a great deal more work than they might think and not a great get-rich-quick plan, and that I never recommend using sex as a way to piss someone off or get revenge.

We document the embodiment of pleasure for folks who are interested in exploring their desires on-screen in a safe setting, and in general the money quickly goes. A performer might make somewhere between $400 to $1200 for their scene, but the producer is making money off of that scene and screening that scene globally for decades after it is shot.

If you are a performer, never commit to a scene you don't believe in or that you are not proud to call your work, because it will never go away. Really. And as a director, don't hire a performer who isn't 100% committed to the scene. It will cost you money in the end and can ruin a film.

If a performer is being honest about only wanting to shoot for money, realize that that is telling you that they don't much care what your vision is for this film or the ethos with which it is produced. That will come across on screen. If your applicant communicates that they are trying to raise money while in college, and they would rather perform and work for other queers and do something radical over the summer that aligns with their social and political beliefs and practices, instead of doing admin work somewhere, then this is a more specific, honest response. It states a need to work and make money, and an alignment with the beliefs and vision of your company, plus a desire to be a part of what you are creating because of that vision.

Being compensated with a fair wage and treated with respect for the work being done is essential for a performer. But the work involved in pornography and erotic film is so much more than punching a clock and showing up. There is a great deal of presence, emotional vulnerability and energy exchanged in the process of performing in an erotic film. If it's not something a performer is committed to emotionally and psychologically, and is solely motivated by a desire for economic gain, it's a recipe for a disaster – it won't create space for the performer's or director's work to thrive, grow or manifest in a way that is aligned with the ethos of feminist and DIY porn making.

It's important to talk with all individuals involved in your production about where the film will be distributed and how many people will see it. Make sure they are comfortable with the fact that their parents or other family or friends might see this film, and that they are comfortable enough around their decision to have that talk, either preemptively or when the time comes.

So once these initial correspondences have happened and you are sitting across the table from your potential performer over coffee, what do you talk about? I like to conduct the interview starting with a description of my company, my values around production, and a basic overview of the next film that I'm casting. Remember, if this person isn't right for a role that you have in this film, they might be excellent for your next film. They might even be interested in being an extra or production assistant to get an insider's view on just what it is like on one of your film sets.

After I have talked with the performer about the project, I like to review what I have learned about them through our email correspondences and application, and keep a photo of them (can be fully clothed), along with their application and my notes from our interview, in a file folder of potential performers.

I might start a conversation like this: " So you went to Smith College and you're new to San Francisco..."

"And you're inspired to be a part of the feminist porn movement because...?

"That's great! It's a pretty exciting movement. Are there any directors or performers that really inspire you? What about them inspires you?

"Do you have anyone in mind who you might like to shoot with in a scene? A performer that you have seen in films, or a partner/lover?

"What about that person really turns you on?

"What would your dream scene involve? What would that look like?

"Hmm, I'd love to see if I could include elements of that. What parts of that fantasy do you find to be really hot?"

Let the performer know if you're having any thoughts about a specific scene that they might be a good fit for. And if there's dialogue in the film and you are unsure of the performer's camera presence, feel free to invite them to an audition.

I have never, as a director, called an audition past the in-person interview. But I try to keep my dialogue very simple, and direct my films in such a way that the acting is not an essential element. Also, I've worked before with most of the performers that I cast, so I have some idea about their acting ability. Keep the dialogue simple if you can. As a performer, I have gone into auditions for films that are dialogue-heavy and where the sex was secondary. Remember, we are telling a story with pictures.

Once you've talked with the performer and you understand their vision and desires as well as their limits and boundaries concerning the film, you can start to incorporate their visions into the film. For example if they are really into cake-sitting and Marilyn Monroe, and you know that one of your scenes is going to happen in the kitchen, you now have a direction for your kitchen scene. Someone is baking a cake and things get messy in the kitchen, perhaps topped off with an iconic Marilyn Monroe style "Happy Birthday" song. You now have direction and a tone, you can even bring in vintage '60s flair that intersects with sploshing – a sexy way to celebrate a lover's birthday. Maybe their partner is a James Dean drag king! Oooh, I'm getting goose bumps. I might have to write that script if you don't!

KNOWING WHAT QUESTIONS TO ASK

Important questions to ask your performers are things like, What is your preferred lube? Do you have any food allergies or food preferences? When were you last tested for STIs, and what safer sex practices would you like to implement for this scene?

Clear communication is important, and truly listening to your performers is key in developing trust. I let my performers know that if fucking in cowboy boots or sneakers makes them feel hot, they should do it! I want performers to feel sexy and appreciated for who they are, not molded into some idea of what we think the audience wants to see. I want to represent them in a way that feels authentic to who they are as sexual beings. If a performer tells me that lilies and dark chocolate make her feel sexy then I will show up (and I have shown up) with lilies and dark chocolate. My performers know that I listen and that I care, and that makes a huge difference.

I know this as a performer as well. I'm vegan, and many times I've gone to a long day of shooting on set in which I'm starving but there is nothing I can eat. One fabulous director who always asks about food preferences is Tristan Taormino. Tristan is a mindful advocate for her performers in many ways, but one of the things I appreciate the most is really having food that I can eat on set. I feel taken care of and nourished, and I'm able to give 100% during my scenes because of it.

One of my DIY porn mentors, my husband James Mogul, reinforced the importance of feeding your models when I first started directing. I never forgot his words: "Your performers will love you if you feed them, and they will verbalize their appreciation." Performing and producing erotic film is hard work and long hours, and if folks get hungry they will end up tired, cranky, irritable and making mistakes. So feed your performers good food. Hire a caterer or get your production assistant to pick up some good Thai food or something fresh. Make sure that you are accommodating everyone's dietary needs and food sensitivities.

REAL SHAG TOP

REAL SHAG TOP is a an acronym I use to remember what to review and discuss within BDSM scene negotiations, and this same acronym can be a helpful tool and reminder for performers in what they might want to negotiate and discuss prior to their scene.

- **R – ROLES.** This is in reference to any *role-play* elements that the performers might want to take on as part of the scene, or any headspace that they might be wanting to explore, such as dominant/submissive, sadist/masochist. It might include the character or role written in the narrative of the script as well, in which case the director will be explaining the character's framework. For example, in one of my films, *Women Reclaiming Sex on Film,* I had two performers who had decided on a narrative and role-play fantasy they wanted to explore: both of the women were dressed in very vintage femme rockabilly style wardrobe. One of the two women, "Bettina Doll," was caught keying another woman's red convertible, and had to be punished and fucked for her wrongdoing.

  It was a fantasy that the two women talked about for months, and we spent ages getting the right location, car and wardrobe, and really making it a perfect scene for the two women. It was Bettina's first porn scene and we wanted it to be truly special. She also wanted to be fisted in the film, and we were able to document that experience for her. The two women really ironed out their well-defined roles prior to the scene, and it was an honor to document.

- **E – EXPECTATIONS.** If a performer says that they are *expecting* a really rough sex scene or they enjoy being a sensation slut, those are very broad terms that can mean a lot of different things to different people. It's important for performers to discuss how they might envision the scene going and what their expectations are. They should talk about specific sex acts or implements they expect or envision being used in the scene, as well as the tone of the scene. Is this a scene that that the performers want to keep light and playful? Slow and sensual? Or rough and aggressive sex that really pushes one another's physical limits? Stating expectations and making sure that all scene partners are on the same page can assist in creating a scene that everyone enjoys.

- **A – ADDRESS.** What *names and pronouns* are being used on set? This is an important question for all the cast and crew. Whether the camera is rolling or not, using everyone's preferred on set/on-camera name is important, so folks don't get confused and use an off-camera name while the camera is rolling. As a director, please make sure that all your cast and crew are using correct pronouns for folks. Sending out a sheet to folks on screen names and pronouns prior to production can be helpful, and making on-set announcements to advocate for correct pronoun usage can be helpful.

  Whether folks are taking on or exploring roles of dominance and submission or not, checking in about how each individual would like to be addressed in the film is important. For example, just because someone is role-playing a dominant/submissive dynamic in a scene doesn't mean that "master" or "slave" are terms that are comfortable for the people in either the dominant or submissive roles. Check in about how each individual does and does not like to be addressed.

- **L – LENGTH, LIKES AND LIMITS.** Knowing how *long* the scene will be really helps performers in pacing themselves. If I'm shooting a feature film, I generally need around thirty-five to forty minutes of footage for the sex scene, which will be edited down to somewhere between fifteen and twenty minutes of footage. This is not including the narrative. I try to shoot approximately twice as much footage as I will need for the final edit. Knowing this, perhaps even giving performers a cue for every five minutes of footage, can be helpful in giving them a better understanding of their pacing during the scene.

Performers discussing their sexual *likes* and *limits* can help you draw a framework of boundaries, and sculpt a scene based on sexual acts and dynamics that really turn them on.

- **S – SAFEWORDS, SAFETY PRECAUTIONS and SEXUAL CONTACT.** Whether performers are engaging in a kink scene or a vanilla scene, safewords can be helpful on set. It's important to be aware of the vulnerability of your performers as they are allowing us into their intimate world. Let the performers know that if they need the camera to stop rolling, they can call CUT, or HOLD if they need us to bring them in water, or more lubricant, or a baby wipe, or if they just need five minutes to compose themselves after a really intense sexual exchange.

  What *safety precautions* are being taken? What type of risks are part of this particular scene? Having a cell phone, first aid kit and safety scissors nearby are all safety precautions. Having a fire extinguisher on set, having water and sunscreen if you are shooting outside, having a production assistant available with shoes or flip-flops and a robe if you are shooting on the beach. Let your performers know about these precautions. You want them to know their health and well-being are of the utmost importance.

  What types of *sexual contact* are the performers comfortable with and interested in exploring in this scene? Oral sex? Toys? Penetration? Vibrators? These expectations, limits and desires surrounding sexual contact should all be addressed between performers prior to the scene and should be shared with the director.

  What safer sex supplies and STD tests are necessary precautions to protecting the health of both performers?

- **H – HEALTH.** Are there any *health* concerns that the performers need to share with the director or other performers? Any recent surgeries? Mobility concerns? Two health concerns that I always communicate on set, which primarily comes up during BDSM shoots, is that I have a heart condition that prevents me from engaging in electrical play, and I have TMJ and my jaw can easily dislocate – so I can rarely do gags, and when I do, not for an extended period of time.

- **A – ALLERGIES, ATTIRE, AFTERCARE.** Knowing if your performer has *allergies* is an important element in casting and directing. For example, if your performer has a cat allergy but you book a venue that has a cat, this could create major difficulties in your filming, and an uncomfortable experience for your model. Knowing food allergies is important in the catering of your shoot, as well as allergies to any materials that might be present at the venue – in the sex toys, safer sex supplies, or anything else that your performer might come in contact with on set.

  Attire – Discussing wardrobe prior to the shoot is key. What do the models need to bring and what will you have on set already? Remember to discuss how many changes of clothes to bring, colors of clothes, style of clothing and footwear. Remind performers to refrain from using clothing with words or logos.

  Aftercare is terminology we use within the BDSM world to refer to the care of someone after a scene, and this pertains to models as well. It's important to make sure that your performers have a good support system set up for after a shoot. After the excitement and endorphin rush of an intense sexual experience, climactic rush and energy downpour, your performers might experience "shoot-drop" – an experience in which they have depleted all their energy and yummy feel-good endorphins, and might need some support in place as they engage in self-care and ground themselves emotionally.

Queer porn star Double H, who stared in my film *Tangled Heart Strings,* talked to me of their aftercare needs, stating, "Different folks need different things to feel good and looked after post-shoot, and this may vary depending on what content you're shooting. As with real-life play and sex, afterwards, I like company, a hot bath, huge amounts of food and a beer or two. And more of everything if I've been bottoming or subbing. Performing in porn was no different. Sometimes I'm super tired but don't want to be alone doing nothing. When I shot for *Tangled Heart Strings,* I was far away from home and I was lucky enough to have a delightful crew to feed me until I was fit to burst, take me out for beers, and then back for sofa snuggles and watching *Harold and Maude* until bedtime."

Feminist porn starlet Siouxsie Q, Double H's co-star in *Tangled Heart Strings,* advises performers to not make concrete plans for after a porn shoot. Siouxsie tells us, "Sometimes when I finish shooting a scene, I want to keep the cum on my face and the eyelashes on my lids and hit the town! I want to ride the wave of endorphins and go out and spend the money I just made on shoes, oysters and champagne. But usually when I finish a shoot, I am ready for a big cheeseburger, my teddy bear, and an endless stream of *Star Trek: The Next Generation* episodes. There's almost no way to predict which version will strike, and when, and I often find myself tempted to say "Oh absolutely! Let's meet up for drinks when I get done shooting on Thursday," but I have learned that it is unwise to commit myself to going out after I have done a full day of sex work. Even when the porn is super fun, silly, creative and feminist, making porn is still hard work and can be incredibly draining."

- **G – GEAR.** What kind of *gear* do your performers need to bring? Any sex toys? Personal lubricant? Props? Their identification for paperwork? A water bottle? Do they need to bring their own makeup, or will there be a makeup artist on the set? Make sure all this is communicated within your negotiations and is present in your call sheet for your performers to refer back to before they pack for their shoot. If everything they need to bring, including wardrobe, is in one email, that makes it much easier to refer back to, rather than fumbling through multiple correspondences.
- **TOP – TYPE OF PLAY.** What *type of play* will your performers be engaging in? Discussing and blocking out the type of play that they plan to explore in the scene will make it easier for both the performers and the crew to document the action.

◆

As you can see from the extensive list above, it is almost as important as the director's conversation with performers to have the performers who are shooting together talking to one another. Sometimes these people might already be lovers or partners, but if they are not, make sure to introduce them and help them along in their correspondence.

An email intro between two performers might look something like this:

> Hello Alice and Tory,
>
> I'm so excited to be working with both of you. I wanted to introduce the two of you and encourage you to connect to discuss your scene before the big day. Some things that you might want to discuss when you meet up are your likes/dislikes, turn-ons, what your favorite positions are, your boundaries, and things that you would

like to try out during the scene. This is also a good time to talk about safer sex, testing and allergies (latex, silicone, etc.). This is a great time to negotiate.

Get inspired and let me know how the conversation goes, so I'm prepared to best facilitate an incredible experience for both of you. Let me know if you have any questions or if I can be of any assistance in further facilitating.

Best,
Madison

Now sometimes folks meet up, and sometimes life happens for busy folks and they talk over Skype, or the phone, or not at all. I try to check up to see how things are developing and whether I can help in matchmaking at all before the shoot.

If folks show up to the shoot and they haven't talked yet, I create space and time for them on set. If I need to, I sit down with them. We will go over some ideas and I'll ask them about their desires and what they are most excited about in this scene. If I get a vague answer like, "I'm excited about being really submissive," I ask, "What does that look like for you?" or, "What about being submissive is the most exciting to you?" Or, "When you step into the fantasy of you being submissive, what exactly are you doing?"

Some people are more comfortable than others at articulating their desires. For some folks it can be a real challenge, and these specific questions, along with active listening, can assist in pulling out the fantasies and desires that your performer will most authentically embody in this scene.

WORDS OF WISDOM FROM POST PORN FEMINIST FILMMAKER MARIA LLOPIS

The work of María Llopis encompasses a variety of forms and media, such as photography, video and performance. She develops her own alternative vision of sexual identity and gender, always based on a strong feminist political position. Llopis deconstructs the sexual subject of feminism in order to develop a discourse that is closer to practices around pro-sex feminism or transfeminism – but above all, Llopis situates sexuality/intimacy as a powerful force of creation and as a necessary political weapon for questioning the society we live in.

1. Do shoot anything you feel like shooting. What I have learned over the years is that it's not about the type of shot, but about *how* it is shot. For example, a cum shot (where the guy comes on a woman's face) may be a boring, non-feminist type of shot, the kind you may feel you want to avoid. But you may shoot it in a different way, with a different perspective, and it may turn upside down – and this change is political. You may, for example, use a non-normative dick. The woman may not

use makeup, or may have a non-normative, non-binary look. You could have this guy with a tiny penis cumming over this great butch woman and both of them having lots of fun later while she fists him in the ass. You are subverting the paradigm of the strong manly guy and the passive lady "receiving."

2. Shoot what you desire. Desire cannot be faked. Shoot your interests, your dreams and your inner fantasies, no matter how strange they may be. Because they are truly yours and therefore not part of a sexist and misogynist industry that wants to tell us what sexual practices we should enjoy or not. Be true to yourself. Perhaps you think that no one else may be interested in having sex with your cactus... only to discover that there are people indeed and that it's a great idea to shoot a queer orgy in a cactus garden.

3. Have fun while remaining political. DIY porn/feminist porn/radical porn is about mixing politics and fun. I have realized with my work over the years that you cannot do feminist politics unless they are part of your own sexuality and body. Postporn and DIY feminist porn are for me the practical side, the flesh and bones of feminist politics. To enjoy the power of our sexuality is political.

4. Embrace change and the unknown. For example: You may feel that parenthood has nothing to do with porn... but it may have. That's what has happened to me, in fact. I had been working for many years in postporn and feminist pornography, but during the last years my interest switched to maternity. And in fact, there is a whole world out there in parenthood regarding our sexuality. Women who have ecstatic/orgasmic births. Women who come when breastfeeding. Trans men who give birth and breastfeed. People who enjoy sexuality and

parenthood and understand that parenthood is a door to a new kind of sexuality.

I am going to publish a book about *Subversive Parenthood* that addresses sexuality in pregnancy and labor, as well as queer parenthood and other themes that I started researching in my DIY feminist porn years.

5. Love. Love yourself, love what you do, your work, your collagues, your camera, your fight, your politics. Respect and honor your body and the bodies of the people you have sex with, in front (and behind) the camera.

10 PRODUCTION FLOW

OFTEN I TRY TO SHOOT AN ENTIRE FILM IN a single day. This is a wildly exhausting experience, and generally means about a fifteen-hour day. But if you're able to make it happen, it really cuts back on your overall budget, and often as a DIY pornographer I'm working with minimal production budgets.

Let's assume I'm doing a single-day shoot. This generally means I'm at the location by 8 a.m. with the crew – my production assistant, gaffer, videographer and photographer – to set up. I'm discussing with my videographer the first shots that we'll be shooting, and describing the lighting and shots so that we're set when we start to roll.

The production assistant is setting up food and a green room for the performers. A green room is an area at the location which you are not shooting in, where you can have food, drinks and snacks set up for your performers. This is a place they can go to relax, get dressed, look over their script, do makeup and prepare for their scene.

The production assistant is also setting out paperwork (see Chapter 11, "Paperwork, Legalities and Obscenity Laws"), and scripts for performers. Then the PA talks with the director about how they want the room set up, and starts to assist with setup of the first shooting location.

Think about everything that you are going to need on set. You want to have everything there and in place, not be running around the venue searching for things once the performers are in place and ready to shoot. Do you have lubricant on set? Are you sure it's the performers' preferred lubricant? Make sure that the performers' preferred lubricant, preferred safer sex supplies – condoms, dental dams and gloves – are all on set and in place – a place that is both convenient for your performers and works for your narrative or aesthetic.

What does the room look like? What sheets are you using? Is the room cluttered with junk or logos and brand names? If you have props to dress the look of the set, explain to your PA what props need to go where, and which items in the room need to be removed. If the "stuff" in your shot doesn't inform your narrative or say something about your characters, then it should be removed from the set. Also look out for brand names and logos. Is there a Coca-Cola can, Juicy Couture pants or bag of Krispy Kreme donuts on the set? Unless you have permission from the company that you are featuring in your shot, you need to remove all logos and brand names from set.

Sometimes lubricant companies will give permission to feature them in your film; otherwise you can use black gaffer tape or vet wrap to cover the name on the bottle. The same goes for gloves or condoms that might be on set. The name and logo shouldn't be recognizable or you might run into potential problems with the company. I have had several friends receive "cease and desist" letters from companies regarding the use of their logo, name or likeness in a film or image, and it really sucks to have to deal with this after production, especially as a small DIY director. So use your eagle eyes beforehand.

Also, having water on set for your performers is important. Sex is physical. You get sweaty and thirsty and you need your coach to run in with a water bottle (or even have one on set if that makes sense), but make sure the labels are removed from the bottles in case one ends up in a shot. Bringing water bottles in and out so they don't end up in a shot is another one of the many duties of my PA. My PA will also be sure to set up extension cords if we need them for vibrators or lights.

Creating a comfortable space for performers on set is key to a successful shoot. If your performers don't feel heard, don't know what is going on or how long they might be waiting around, what the expectations of them are, or what they should be doing, or if they are hungry, nervous, or in need of some reassurance as individuals who are about to share something very intimate with the world, then the scene – and the performers' experience – will suffer.

As a new director, you will probably have some anxieties. Whenever we do things for the first time we might feel a bit nervous, and if you are a performer and/or a director you might feel especially nervous. My advice is to not share that anxiety with your performers. You need to have a PA or other crew support person who can be your go-to: someone who is making sure that you are meeting your self-care needs, such as feeding and watering yourself and taking breaths. If you're still feeling anxious, excuse yourself to the bathroom for a few minutes to relax, think about the situation and come back to your vision and values. You can then bounce the situation off of your support person, and solve the problem with your crew, by adapting and making any necessary changes. If you engage with your own personal self-care throughout your long production day, you can be more present as a support for your performers.

All of these conversations prior to the shoot aid in the comfort of the performer on set. When the performer arrives, we welcome them to the location and offer to help them with any bags they might be toting. I then give a tour of the space, showing them the room we will be shooting in and explaining how I envision that based on our conversations. I show the performer the bathroom and the green room where they can relax, show them where the food is and let them know if any food is specifically earmarked for them, and offer them a water. Often, if it's a morning shoot, I also take coffee orders the night before (or my PA will do this) from all the crew and our morning performers, so that their coffee order is there when they arrive.

I'll show the performer where their packet of paperwork is (including a release and 2257 form, script, and schedule of scenes for the day), and ask them to fill out their paperwork after they settle in. I tell them to relax and let them know I'll be back in a few minutes to go over wardrobe. At this time I also generally ask them for two US government-issued IDs, so that I can have the photographer photograph them for our records. I'll let them know what wardrobe pieces we might need first if there are multiple wardrobe changes, or if I'm shooting still lingerie photos or such beforehand. I also let the performer know when the makeup artist (if there is one) will be ready for them.

I thank the performer for being here, and let them know how excited we are to work with them, and tell them to let us know if they have any questions.

If there are multiple performers performing together, this is also a great time for the them to have a chance to talk further, get to know one another more – if they don't already – and discuss the scene further.

While the performer(s) are settling in, I check in on how set-up is going. What does the lighting look like? Do we have enough light for photos and video? I have the photographer and videographer (which is sometimes me) take test photos and footage with the video camera to see what it looks like, and make any adjustments that are needed. I hand the photographer the performers' IDs to photograph for our 2257 US regulation compliance. Some producers also have the photographer take a photo of the performers holding their IDs. The 2257 US regulation states that the performers need to have their IDs on-set for shooting, so the photo of the them holding their IDs acts as a verification that this regulation was met.

If things are running behind, let your performers know. Sometimes one performer will be late while another is there and waiting around. If you are able to shoot some of your promotional images while waiting for the other performer, or any solo shots of the performer who is there, that can often really help you to not fall too far behind schedule.

When I return to the performer with their IDs, I check in with them and see how they are doing, and look over their paperwork to make sure they've filled everything in correctly. Always make sure to have all parts of the paperwork filled out. Often, performers will turn in partially completed paperwork, and then you have to chase after them post-production to acquire the missing parts, and it's a royal pain in the neck.

Next, I look over wardrobe with the performer. I've had performers who bring everything but the kitchen sink, in enormous pieces of luggage filled with dozens of outfits, and then I've had performers bring a handful of clothing, none of which goes together. Clear communication prior to the shoot about what you need a performer to bring for wardrobe can really help. Sometimes performers are traveling from out of town, so if you email them with a wardrobe list the night before they might already be on tour or on the road, and whatever they left the house with is what they have.

Sometimes having a few wardrobe items in your production kit that you bring with you can be helpful for wardrobe emergencies. I have a lime green hoodie that looks awesome on camera; it has saved me many a time, and shows up in several of my films. A few times recently when I have directed more heavily stylized art house films, I hired a production manager who could double as our wardrobe stylist.

When going through wardrobe with your performer, remember again to avoid clothing with visible logos or brand names. Also, even though many people's wardrobes consist mainly of black, colors actually photograph much better. Be mindful of what colors are in the room you are shooting in: what color is the bedspread or couch? What color palette will the performers be up against? At the same time, consider your performers' characters, and what the performers feel comfortable and sexy in. If your performer is having a hard time deciding between a couple of pieces, ask them which one they feel the most comfortable, confident and sexy in. I've watched a smile comes across a performer's face as they look in the direction of the wardrobe piece that makes them feel that way. That is always the one to go with.

A performer of mine once showed up with a very small bag of clothes, all of which were black or had text on them, but she was wearing these great old-skool tennis shoes and had brought in a bright blue skateboard. I ran the idea by the performer – Missy Minx – of utilizing her awesome skateboard as a prop/wardrobe. I offered Missy my lime green hoodie and hot pink sunglasses, and she posed with her beloved skateboard. We shot some beautiful photographs and videos of Missy out on our venue's rooftop. The colors were amazing and the images and footage really reflected who Missy is, with her sexy California-cool look.

Once you've picked out wardrobe, you can discuss with your performer or performers their scene and what their thoughts and ideas are for it. This gives you all a chance to state out loud your ideas, desires and expectations, and to organize and clarify the order and flow of what exploring the involved positions, toys or sexual acts might look like. The discussion might sound something like this:

"So I see that you have brought some toys. Do you know which ones you might want to try out today?"

"Well, I really love getting fucked with a strap-on after some fingers and oral sex. This is probably my favorite dildo to get fucked with."

"Great. And what positions do you enjoy most when you are being fucked with a strap-on?"

"Oooh, Hmmm, I don't know. Um, I guess I really like it when I'm kind of standing up but leaning over, like this. I also really love spooning and doggie. Oh, and sometimes it's really nice if I can be spanked a little or have my hair pulled a little while I'm in that position."

"And do your prefer these positions for vaginal penetration or for anal play, or what feels best for you?"

"Hmmm. Maybe a little of both. Could we do some vaginal first and then maybe a little anal toward the end?"

"Great. Can you make sure to communicate what kind of stimulation and where you're wanting the cock during the sex scene?"

"Like, in between cuts, or on film?"

"On film."

"Oh, okay. I like that."

"And how about condoms and lube?"

"Yes, let's do condoms on the dildo. It'll just help keep everything clean, and I like the silicone lube. For vaginal and anal. Oh, and I really like to suck cock too. Can we do that a little in the beginning?"

"Sounds good to me. What position do you like to be in for cocksucking?"

"On my knees is my favorite. My gag reflex is a little sensitive, so just let me be in control for the cock sucking, okay? I can really get into it then. That's my favorite."

"And are you hoping to use the Hitachi Magic Wand?"

"Oh, that would be awesome. Can I use that at the very end and have you fuck me with your hands?"

"Gloves or no gloves?"

"Gloves, please. I'm not allergic to latex, so the latex or nitrile gloves work for me. Oh, and sometimes I squirt. Is that okay?"

"Yeah, totally. What position is most comfortable for you?"

"Probably on my back with my legs back."

"Awesome. Sounds good. Remember you can ask for lube and give lots of honest feedback throughout the scene, and these are just markers for where we might start and end the scene. It's totally fine to improv throughout, and we don't have to tick all these things off a list. It's just a structure – a container for us to play within – so don't feel like you have to move on to another position just when things are feeling really good. You're a rock star and we are going to totally have a blast."

"What if I need a break, like water or to cut for a break or pee or something?"

"Just say in an audible volume for both me and the camera, 'Break'. You can break at any time."

Getting assorted angles by climbing up on furniture, as well as getting low to the ground, allows for variation in perspective.

"Oh, and I mean... what if I can't orgasm with the camera rolling? Do you want me to fake an orgasm? I'm a little nervous whether I'll be able to orgasm with a camera on me."

"No, you totally don't need to orgasm or fake an orgasm. Sex can be fun and pleasurable with or without orgasm, with or without ejaculation. Just keep it real and authentic to you and how you're feeling in the moment. The camera person will move around us, and caring for you and your comfort is the most important thing on this set, so if you need anything during the production just let us know."

I've had this conversation as a director and performer dozens of times, and these conversations are absolutely key to creating the space for an amazing scene in which we are honoring, celebrating and documenting individual sexual desire.

After having this conversation, it can be a great idea to block out the scene on set, which should be ready by then. First just block out the scene with movements (you don't have to actually perform the sexual acts at this time – just block out the dance, the way your bodies will be moving – see if the performers need more support, more pillows, is there anything they think they might want based on the blocking? This is also really helpful for the videographer and photographer, as they will be able to figure out their positions and angles for the shot.

Then, depending on the comfort of the performers, you could have them block out the sex positions, actually lightly exploring and dabbling in each position – starting off with making out, undressing, etc. – and the photographer can take photos of each position. During the photos, the models are moving slowly. This is a great time for a lot of slowness, intimacy, eye contact and connection. Remember, you also want to grab photos that are non-nude, that will work for things like movie posters, DVD covers or promotional images.

Now the performers are going to be warmed up and revved up. They have a rhythm and blocking for the dance they are about to experience. They might need their makeup touched up. The lights are set. The videographer is ready. The performers are ready. The director is ready. Now it's time to call "Action!" and get the camera rolling.

"Action!" the director calls, and the beautiful dance begins. You or your videographer is behind the camera and the images are looking gorgeous. You have mostly natural light spilling in through the window, and your performers look other-worldly, like erotic fairy nymphs exploring one another's bodies. They know the dance and they trust you and your crew; now you are simply a wildlife photographer trying not to disturb your performers' environment, their habitat – trying to document some of the beauty that comes from supporting and listening to people's sexual desires and holding space for that expression to come alive.

Your camera frames their faces that are coupled in a gentle kiss. You hold the shot for ten seconds, then move to a frame that encompasses their faces and bodies. You hold for ten seconds, then move to a shot from the point of view of one of the performers: you're positioned over her shoulder, her hand firmly pushes her partner into a lying position on the mattress. You hold for ten seconds, capture an overwhelming smile that blooms on the woman's face before her plump lips are enveloping her partner's fingers, sucking on them – first slowly, then with ravenous hunger. You switch positions to the view point of the woman whose fingers are being sucked, so now we see the absolute joy on the woman's face as she removes her hand from her partner's mouth and traces her fingers down her own body to her cunt. The dance continues, alternating angles and perspectives, lingering on a stable shot for ten seconds before moving on to the next.

Things to have in your production tool kit/production box:

- Lube
- Baby wipes
- Towels
- Snacks

- Bottles of water
- A takeout menu or food prep for the day of shooting
- Sex toys
- Backup wardrobe items that might come in handy
- Any props that are specific to your shoot
- Paperwork – scripts, shot lists, schedule, model releases, 2257 forms
- Checkbook
- Pens
- Sheets
- Robes
- Toiletries if folks are going to need to shower
- Any decorative items for set dressing
- Camera/s
- Chargers
- Batteries for cameras (make sure batteries are fully charged prior to shoot – good to have a minimum of two video camera batteries)
- SD cards
- SD card reader
- Laptop (with charger)
- Hard drive
- Safer sex supplies (gloves, condoms, dental dams)
- A makeup kit
- Makeup wipes
- Douche
- Enema bottles

- Nail file
- Fingernail polish remover
- Gaffer tape
- Vet wrap
- Tripod and/or mono pod
- Extension cord
- Basic light kit and reflector

DISABILITY INCLUSIVE DIY PORN TIPS, BY SHANNA KATZ, M.Ed, ACS

Shanna Katz is a southwest based Board Certified Sexologist who provides sassy, dynamic, fun loving, crowd-pleasing, witty and amusing sexuality education. From academic discussions on body positivity and sexual freedom and corporate trainings on inclusivity and accessibility to fun-filled workshops, she covers the spectrum of sexuality in her work. Currently, Shanna is working on her PhD, with an emphasis on sexuality and marginalized communities.

1. *Don't assume – always ask.* Just because you've worked with a ________ performer before (fill in the blank: Deaf, wheelchair user, mobility impaired, blind, anxious, etc.) doesn't mean that another performer with the same identity or disability is going to need the same things or want to be treated in the same way. When booking talent, always ask some sort of question around accommodations needed, and identities/labels that feel most authentic. When we as society think about accommodations, we tend to think about wheelchair access, and

stop there. Allowing performers to tell you what *their* needs are ensures that you don't forget to have an extra seat for their ASL interpreter during pre-performance discussions or after the shoot dialogue, or to make sure you have a quiet space for them to decompress if they are feeling overly stimulated. You never know if you don't ask, and due to the stigma against disability, many folks may feel as though they don't have the space to make these requests for fear of getting fired or cancelled on. Make sure you ask these questions of *all* performers, even if you have worked with them before. Many disabilities are not visible, and targeting only "obviously" disabled folks is ableist too.

2. *Be Proactive.* Think about the space(s) you are shooting in before you book your performers, and give them a heads-up about what the space looks like/feels like before day of. For example, if you are shooting in a space that doesn't have bathrooms/has bathrooms that aren't mobility accessible/has bathrooms on the other side of the moon, let your performers know that, so they can make educated decisions about a) whether they can even do the shoot, and b) how much liquid they may want to consume beforehand. If you are shooting somewhere that isn't accessible via public transit, and your performers may need to find an accessible cab or get a ride, let them know. Shooting right next to a construction zone that has noises which may trigger PTSD or a migraine? Include that in your pre-shoot info list. The more information you give your performers in advance, the better prepared they can be to give you the best shoot possible.

3. *Be Inclusive.* In my last tip, I mentioned informing folks about your space before they show up, and this goes hand in hand. While it can be difficult finding spaces to shoot your awesome porn (and I get this), do your best to find accessible spaces. This means spaces that aren't up or

down stairs, that have parking lots and/or are close to accessible transit (this means *not* a subway stop that doesn't happen to have an escalator or stairs), that have bathrooms whose doors are wide enough to allow in a wheelchair or crutches, that are supportive of companion or service animals, that aren't incredibly noisy or near strong fumes, that don't have flashing lights, etc. Some of these things you can control (shoot some performers with those awesome strobes you just found, and turn them off for others), but other things you just can't change. When your studio is on a fourth-floor walk-up, what you are saying to performers who cannot use stairs for whatever reason is "I don't care enough about having you in my work to figure out a more accessible option." If that sounds callous, so be it, but it is true. Offering to find someone to carry them up the stairs is not an acceptable alternative (unless the performer requests it on their own). And not everyone is ready to offer ability diverse porn... and that's okay. Just be open about it, instead of saying you want people of all abilities, and then offering spaces that just aren't accessible.

4. *Get Ready to Be Impressed.* I say this, not because people with disabilities and disabled folks are magical special snowflakes, or because we are inspirational solely because we are sexual, hot, horny beings "despite" our disabilities. I say this because we, as people with disabilities, are scrappy and we are creative. Can't hold onto this sex toy because she lacks muscle control in her hand? Watch her figure out how to use another body part, or even duct tape it to body. Can't wield traditional impact toys because of the strength needed? Behold the brilliance of some creative predicament bondage. Can't see his submissive because he is blind? Experience his submissive wearing a bell on his collar so his dominant knows exactly where he is every time he moves. The

list goes on; the number of sex hacks disabled folks have invented to make their sexual experiences turn out as fabulously as they want them to is amazing. Often times, able-bodied and neurotypical folks make assumptions about how crips (a word that has been reclaimed by many disabled people, myself included) have sex, and usually, these expectations are blown out of the water when the cameras start. Of course, it is always nice to have various pillows/wedges/etc. on hand for modifying positions as needed, and having duct tape on set is always a smart idea, but frequently, your performers will already have modified their props to have the hot sex they know and love.

5. *Be Ready to Fuck Up.* It's going to happen. Identity work is tough; power, privilege and oppression are so ingrained in society, and therefore in us, that it is incredibly hard to re-center our minds about the idea that disability isn't a "Bad Thing" (shout out to crip activist Stella Young), and rather, that disability, like gender, sexual orientation, race, ethnicity, and all other identities, is just part of the beautiful variance of humanity. You *will* mess up. You will use some ableist language (lame, crazy, insane, etc.) in front of someone. You will think something is accessible, and it is not. You will perpetuate a microaggression against someone who is disabled (yes, even if you are disabled yourself). I tell you this because it will happen, and when it does, you will feel like shit, and likely, you will feel defensive (especially if it is someone else pointing it out). The best thing you can do in this situation is to acknowledge it ("Yep, I just did that/said that, and it was not okay"), apologize ("I'm sorry that I did that/said that, and will do my best *not* to do it again"), and then, move on. That's the hard part. We often want to have a long discussion about why it happened, or our intent versus the impact it had, or how our one friend does it and that's why

it is okay. Stop. Put it down and move on. When we spend so much time and energy apologizing or explaining away why we were still a good person even though we just did ______, we are not putting it back on the person who was impacted, which isn't fair. Feel free to do your work on educating yourself or decompressing the situation later on with someone you are close to, but for now, just acknowledge, apologize, and move on, so you can get back into shooting that super hot porn, which is the reason you're all there in the first place.

11 PAPERWORK, LEGALITIES AND OBSCENITY LAWS

I'D LIKE TO START THIS CHAPTER BY SAYING THAT I am not a lawyer. I'd like to follow up that statement by saying that if you do not already have a lawyer you trust who is – ideally – familiar with the adult industry and/or entertainment industry, then I highly recommend you seek one out. There are several established adult film industry law firms.

I also highly recommend using the Kink Aware Professionals website as a resource to find the right lawyer for you. You can find the Kink Aware Professionals listing on the National Coalition for Sexual Freedom website: www.ncsfreedom.org.

Once you have found a lawyer you know and trust, they can be a resource for you in everything from setting up a small business to helping you navigate through laws pertaining to the production and distribution of pornography.

One of the most important federal regulations you will need to read thoroughly and consult with a lawyer about is the 2257 US gov-

Performer Elizabeth Thorn sips tea and fills out her paperwork before we start shooting on the set of *Bibliophile.*

ernment regulation. Regulation 2257 is an administrative law meant to enforce the Child Protection and Obscenity Act. The best place to read up on this regulation is FreeSpeechCoalition.com. The FSC web site is also the best place to find the necessary 2257 forms.

Once you become familiar with the basic legalities it won't be difficult, but there are a few things to keep in mind. If you are a director within the United States and your films are distributed in the United States, you need to be in compliance with all US government regulations. Within the United States, you may not shoot performers who do not have a valid US government-issued ID.

If you are traveling outside of the United States and shooting a model from outside of the United States, you simply keep on file the ID that is their country's equivalent. A passport is generally good as a primary ID, but again, it is not legal to shoot that same model (if they don't have a valid US government-issued ID) within the United States.

You need to obtain photos of models' IDs. Ideally it is good to have two IDs, as well as a photo of your model holding these IDs. This image of your model holding the IDs proves that the IDs were actually physically on-set during the production.

The model release and the 2257 regulation form are two different forms. The model release is a legal document stating your rights of usage to the material in which your performer has just performed. The 2257 form is to make sure you stay within federal compliance.

If you are hoping for your film to be picked up by a distributor or purchased by a larger production house, it is very helpful to have a lawyer look over your contract. On the first several films that I directed, I was so excited to have them picked up by a distributor that I rushed into the process and signed the contract without really understanding what it said or meant. I signed it right away, and in doing so, signed away my rights to those first few films. I got myself into what was, financially, a pretty unfortunate deal. I lived and I learned. That is truly a part of DIY.

Companies generally are advocating for themselves and not their artists, which is unfortunate. I have certainly worked with some producers who were incredible, and who did truly advocate for the wellbeing and vision of their directors. But before rushing into signing a contract, take a breath and look it over with a lawyer to truly understand the ins and outs of what you are agreeing to. Understand the artist's payment structure, distribution and ownership of your film and material.

Obscenity laws are another legal element pertaining to the creation of DIY porn, and this is another area in which it is helpful to have a lawyer. There are certain sexual activities that are risky for distribution and billing, and at high risk for obscenity charges. These include any sexual activities that include blood – menstrual blood, or rough sex within a BDSM scene – such as anal or vaginal sex in which blood appears. In some states, female ejaculate is considered obscene. I've had billing companies request that I edit out religious iconography, such as when I was bound to and suspended from to a cross. My billing processor – CC Bill – requested that I edit out any wide shots of the actual cross.

I also filmed an erotic interpretation of Shakespeare's *Macbeth,* in which witches engage in knife and blood play. Blood also appears during the murder of Banquo, and the moment in which Lady Macbeth takes her life. We were quite explicit in our behind-the-scenes footage about the fact that the film is fictional, outlining the safety precautions we took to keep all performers safe, but our billing processor rejected the film and we had to find an alternate payment processor for it.

In some instances bondage with penetrative sex, or bondage with penis/vagina penetration, is considered too obscene. Fisting is generally considered obscene (however, four fingers or even eight fingers is okay). Pee and poo are taboo as well. But many things, like context and distribution, factor into these issues.

Will this film just be screened at a film festival? Is it part of a documentary or a fantasy narrative? Does the film have artistic or educational merit? Are you marketing the film as erotic art, erotic film or porn? Is the film on DVD and are you shipping it to Alabama or Florida? Does it contain hardcore anal fisting with a girl in bondage?

Regardless of where the film is going, it is good to have a lawyer to consult with, and have all your legal documents in place. Even if it's a film that you and your partner are creating just for the two of you, make an agreement of consent, outlining what you are consenting to, and stating that the film will only be accessible on your hard drive or on a DVD that doesn't leave the house.

So where does 2257 compliance information show up within your records and media? First, there are your paper and digital records. If you have a website, your 2257 information is on the front page. If you have a box cover for your film, the compliance statement and relevant information are on the back of the box cover. There will also be a compliance statement at the beginning of your film, before the credits.

Remember, the work you're doing is important, and it's also controversial. It's important to know the law and to have legal advocates in place prior to moving forward in your film practice, and to have a legal advocate on speed-dial for if/when you need them.

RELEASE FORM AND WORK FOR HIRE AGREEMENT

For good and valuable consideration, the receipt and sufficiency of which is hereby acknowledged by the parties to this Agreement,

Artist: ____ Print name ("Artist"), and

Producer: ________________________ ("Producer"), hereby agree to the following as of

Date: ____________________: **Compensation to Artist**: $____________

Name of Project: ____ ("Project") is tentatively the name of the work or project for which the Artist is rendering services, but such name may change at Producer's discretion.

Artist's Services: Artist agrees to render services in connection with the creation of video, audio, audiovisual, photographic, textual and/or computer generated works. These services may include, without limitations, acting, performing, modeling, voice-over, pre-production, post production services, and/or services as a photographer, videographer, choreographer, designer, director, composer, musician, vocalist, engineer or other agreed-upon services. Artist shall at all times render services in a professional and timely manner, and use best efforts to perform all services to the best of Artist's ability exclusively for Producer until Project completion, as determined by Producer. Services to be rendered by Artist shall also include any and all retakes and remakes, and all voice-overs, scans, re-scans, samples and other pre-production and post-production services requested by Producer relating to the Project. Producer shall not be obligated to compensate Artist if Artist does not render the services under this Agreement or if the Project or the shoot is cancelled for any reason.

Consent: Artist expressly consents and agrees that Producer, and all of Producer's agents or assignees may film, videotape, record, photograph, digitally sample, and otherwise fix in any and all tangible media of expression now known or hereinafter invented all services rendered hereunder, including without limitation all performances, poses and all associated information, including, Artist's image, likeness, voice, bodily sounds and other characteristics of Artist's persona and personality. Artist expressly consents to all such fixations of Artist clothed, partially clothed, costumed, and fully nude. Artist acknowledges and agrees that Artist's performance hereunder may be considered "XXX" sexual activity.

Work For Hire: Artist hereby agrees that all of the works, including without limitation, all audiovisual works, movies and scenes of every kind for which Artist or Artist's employees or agents provide any services pursuant to this Agreement, ("Works") shall immediately and automatically become the exclusive property of Producer as a *work made for hire* as defined by U.S. Copyright Law. The works produced hereunder may be freely edited by, assigned, sold and/or otherwise exploited in any manner by Producer.

Derivative Works: Producer shall at all times have the unfettered right to create and exploit in any manner Derivative Works. The term "Derivative Work," as used in this Agreement, shall mean any and all compilations, derivations, modifications, alterations, synthetic creations, synthespian creations, recreations, alterations, enhancements, superimpositions, recombinations, and distortions of the works, scenes, movies and/or derivative works thereof by any means or process now known or hereinafter developed.

Products: Artist agrees that all photographs and videos of her face, image and body, whether clothed, partially clothed or fully nude and her stage name may be used in perpetuity by Producer, Producer's agents, licensee's and assigns on the packaging and advertising of

This is what a model release might look like.

products that are sexually explicit, including, but, not limited to, vibrators, dongs, dildos, breasts and other body parts, dolls and marital aids.

Ownership Of Resulting Intellectual Property: Artist expressly agrees that Producer shall be the sole and exclusive owner of all rights, title and interest, of every kind and character, in and to all Works and Derivative Works, including, without limitation, all intellectual property rights. The unlimited and absolute grant of rights in Works and Derivative Works to Producer herein is in perpetuity, for all time, cannot be revoked, and includes, without limitation, the following rights: The perpetual and unlimited rights throughout the universe to copy, reproduce, duplicate, exhibit, publish, broadcast, transmit, distribute, perform, promote, license, sell and otherwise use and exploit the Works and Derivative Works by any and all means and methods now known or hereafter discovered, devised or invented, in every and all media, including, without limitation DVDs, VHS, CD-ROM, cable, satellite, broadcast, wide area computer networks, including the Internet, mobile phones, theatrical, print, and computer game media and the unlimited right to use Artist's names, one or more fictitious names generated by Producer, or no name, and the right to use Artist's likeness, voice, persona and other characteristics, on, in and in connection with any and all uses of Works and Derivative Works, including, without limitation, on, in and in association with, goods and services of every kind, including, sex toys, advertisements, synthetically created works, digital actor works, synthespian works and other synthetic creations of all kinds thereof, created by any and all means now known or hereinafter created.

Waiver of Moral Rights: Artist hereby expressly and forever waives all of Artist's moral rights arising under 17 U.S.C. §106A, including all similar or analogous rights arising under all laws.

Waiver of Liability: Artist hereby releases, discharges and agrees to hold harmless Producer and all persons lawfully deriving authority from the Producer, including without limitation, Producer's employees, agents, contractors, performers, service providers, affiliates, financiers and licensees, from any and all claims or liability arising out of, relating to or resulting from the services performed hereunder, including any and all sexually transmitted diseases, conditions or ailments. Artist acknowledges that Artist is not required as a condition of employment by Producer to engage in any actual sexual conduct in the course of the performance or otherwise, and that any such sexual conduct or contact between Artist and any other person(s), if it should occur, is exclusively a result of Artist's own exclusive choice, decision and assumption of risk. Artist further acknowledges that Producer has made no representations to Artist as to the health of any performer, or that any other performer or actor is free from any communicable or transmissible disease, including without limitation, sexually transmitted diseases.

Artist's Warranties: Artist hereby warrants that (i) Artist is over the age of eighteen (18) years; (ii) that all medical, identification and age verification documentation which Artist presents to Producer are, at all times, true, unaltered, genuine, and valid; and (iii) Artist is legally free to execute this Agreement.

Independent Contractor: Artist agrees that Artist is performing as an independent contractor and is responsible to take care of Artist's own tax liability incurred by this Agreement.

Miscellaneous: This Agreement shall be construed in accordance with, and governed by, the laws of the State of California. Any and all disputes of any kind arising out of or relating to this Agreement shall be submitted to final and binding arbitration. THE PARTIES HEREBY WAIVE ANY RIGHTS THEY MAY HAVE TO A TRIAL BY JURY, AND INSTEAD CHOOSE TO RESOLVE THEIR DISPUTES BY ARBITRATION. This Agreement embodies the entire agreement between Artist and Producer on the subject matter referenced herein and that all prior representations, warranties, promises and agreements between the parties which are not expressly included in this Agreement shall be of no force or effect. The parties agree that this Agreement shall be binding upon the parties and their heirs, legal representatives, and assigns. Each party has had the opportunity to consult legal counsel prior to signing this Agreement.

ARTIST'S SIGNATURE FULL LEGAL NAME

PRODUCER'S SIGNATURE

This is what Page 2 of a model release might look like.

RECORDS KEEPING COMPLIANCE FORM PURSUANT TO 18 U.S.C. § 2257

MODEL IDENTIFYING INFORMATION AND AFFIDAVIT: Model understands that all the information given in this Agreement is being provided to comply with federal law and any false statement will subject Model to both a civil action by Producer as well as criminal prosecution under federal and state law _______ (Model's Initials)

Legal Name: ____
(Full Current Legal Name First, Middle, Last)

Date of Birth: ________________ Age: _____
(Month, Day, Year)

Primary identification document must be government issued passport, driver's license, motor vehicle department ID, or military ID. (Each should be described, including the ID number. Clear, good-quality photocopies of each must be attached to this Form and the photocopies must be signed in ink by Model.)

(1) First form of identification: (2) Second form of identification:

______________________________ ______________________________

ID # __________________________ ID # __________________________

All other names previously used (legal names, stage names, aliases and nicknames):

____

____

Phone Number: ____

Mailing Address: ____

This is what a 2257 regulation form looks like.

SWORN STATEMENT: "UNDER 28 U.S.C. § 1746 AND THE PENALTIES OF PERJURY UNDER THE LAWS OF THE UNITED STATES, I SWEAR THAT THE FOREGOING IS TRUE AND CORRECT AND THAT EACH OF THE IDENTIFICATION DOCUMENTS WHICH I HAVE PROVIDED AND OF WHICH I HAVE SIGNED THE ATTACHED COPY WAS LAWFULLY OBTAINED BY ME AND HAS NOT BEEN FORGED OR ALTERED."

Signature:______________________________ Today's Date: __________
(Model's Signature)

SWORN STATEMENT: "UNDER 28 U.S.C. § 1746 AND THE PENALTIES OF PERJURY UNDER THE LAWS OF THE UNITED STATES, I SWEAR THAT I BELIEVE THE FOREGOING IS TRUE AND CORRECT, THAT I HAVE PERSONALLY EXAMINED THE MODEL'S PHOTO IDENTIFICATION AND DATE OF BIRTH, AND THAT I HAVE OBSERVED THE ORIGINALS OF EACH OF THE IDENTIFICATION DOCUMENTS OF WHICH COPIES ARE ATTACHED HERETO AND SIGNED BY THE MODEL."

Signature:______________________________ Today's Date: __________
(Signature of Primary Witness)

____
(Print Name of Primary Witness)

Copy of Depiction Attached:

Hardcopy/Digital: ____

Internet Location/URL:____

Other requests/specifications for publication of images, identities used, etc. may be listed below and initialed by all parties involved:

This is what Page 2 of a 2257 regulation form looks like.

12 SHOOTING STYLES & ANGLES

GREAT NEWS REGARDING EQUIPMENT, MY DIY PORN makers! You can shoot film festival quality films with a camera as simple as the one on your smart phone. It's true! I have seen beautiful films that have been screened at HUMP Festival, and films that have won Feminist Porn Awards, that were shot on an iPhone. I've also shot footage for some of my films on iPhones and flip-cams that cost under $200.

I mention this because it is easy to get wrapped up in the idea that better, fancier, more expensive gear will make your film better. But this is not the case. The important thing is finding a camera that feels like a natural extension of your body.

Find a camera that you know how to use, or can learn how to use, and that assists you, not distracts you, in your creative process. Don't get so involved in fancy camera moves and techniques that you forget about the people in front of the lens. There's always new equipment coming out, advancing technology in media-making. The important thing is to get a camera – even if it's the one on your phone – and really learn how to use it. Learn how to manipulate it, how to create the images that you want using the equipment you have. If your camera is new, make sure to make time to practice shooting with your camera before you are on set. You don't want to be concerned with learning new equipment while you're working.

Earlier in this book, we discussed how to create a shot list. That shot list is a guide for you and your videographer (who might also be you) for capturing the images you want to string together to create your film. I generally suggest shooting all your narrative components, including interviews, prior to the sex scene. Sometimes you can actually shoot this on a separate day, depending on budget, performer and crew availability. If you are shooting all in one day, I do recommend shooting the narrative and dialogue prior to sex. You know how you feel post-orgasm? How it's difficult to remember your name after really great sex? Well, imagine having to deliver lines post-orgasm. It's really difficult, and will take so much longer to get through narrative and dialogue shots if you try to do them after sex. So just don't do it.

Also, if you've built any extensive interviews of individuals or couples into your film, make sure to do that pre-sex as well. Your performers will be much more articulate in their responses, and this also gives them time to get into sex headspace prior to the sex by talking about themselves, their desires, their sexual identity, etc. Also, filming the interviews first allows more time for the performers to get to know one another if they aren't already well acquainted. If you are looking for a blissed-out post sex interview with very basic responses about what they enjoyed in the sex scene, that can be a nice addition. But after a sex scene it's nice to really give performers come-down time, and not ask them a bunch of questions.

When it comes to shooting sex, I am a wildlife photographer. Each director and videographer will have their own style, but I like to be close to the action, not far away and zooming in. I strive to create space in which the performers can connect with one another, and for the most part, allow the presence of the videographer, director and crew to disappear (or for the energy of the crew and director to support the energy of the scene).

When I'm shooting sex, I'm generally shooting with a single camera, and I use the thirty-second technique. This means I find my shot, my frame, my photo, and I stay on that frame for thirty seconds. Once I've come to a stable shot, I count to thirty in my head. First I'll have a full frame, meaning a frame that contains my subjects and the set. Then I'll get a shot of the action, say a kiss or a spank on the bottom, or one woman's hand moving in to touch another's. Then I'll move to a shot of the reaction to that action, like a close face shot of a reaction from the point of view of the receiver, or over the shoulder of the person doing the action. Then I get a reaction shot of the person who's doing the action, then back out to a full frame.

I'll bounce around in this pattern, alternating angles, shooting from a low angle or down from a high angle, and holding each shot, each picture, each frame, for a count of thirty. These should be shots that you are finding within the action of the sex. Remember to facilitate space for the general blocking of the sex so you have an idea of the action, but do not try to call out or orchestrate whose hand is going where at what moment. Allow your performers to develop their groove without you interfering. You want for them to feel connected to one another, not worried about whether they are giving you the performance you're expecting. If there is something terribly distracting or that is totally ruining the shot, call "Hold," so that you can make the adjustment you need, or "Cut," if you need to cut from filming and give further direction.

With this method of shooting, I only use a single camera. I believe that the fewer bodies on set the better, and I think that more than one camera on a set is just overkill. If I have one videographer, or if I'm shooting and know the shots I need, there's no need for more than one videographer.

The only exception to the one-videographer guideline is if I need to call in the photographer to do still photographs, or if I have a production assistant grabbing behind-the-scenes shots for social media.

Sometimes I have our PA on set live-Tweeting images from the shoot; followers often get very excited by a rush of photos live from on set. If you are able to include a link to pre-sales of the film, you could generate some sales before you've finished shooting the film. If you decide to broadcast the shooting process live, then you might need a second videographer shooting the behind-the-scenes live broadcast. If you do have more camera-wielding bodies in the room, you need to be sure that they don't get in your primary videographer's shot. That is the key footage; everything else is secondary.

Another method of shooting that I have experienced involves three cameras. I directed a few films for the company Girlfriend's Films, and they shoot in this manner. The producer has a very specific way in which he likes his films shot and always uses this method. The technique of three cameras involves having all three cameras on tripods, set up in a triangular format surrounding the action. One camera captures the full wide-frame of the subjects, the second camera is on the action (spanking, fucking, licking, sucking, etc.), and the third is capturing reaction shots. Three cameras means a lot more footage to sort through and more syncing of audio. Using a director's clapboard for all the cameras to sync to is important in this modality. Shooting with three cameras also means that you have more extensive coverage of every aspect of the sex scene. But I find it to be a more complicated process and an excess of footage that I simply don't need to tell the story. Having three cameras also means needing three camera operators or three videographers, which triples your budget line item for videographers, cameras and tripods. If you do choose to use multiple cameras, be aware that you'll need to sync up their color balance, so it's best to work with the same camera make and model so that splicing between footage isn't jarring (unless that's the look you are going for).

Early in my DIY porn-making career, I ran into a situation in which I needed to use a completely different camera for the second half of a scene. I was shooting the third scene and second location of the day for my film Writers and Rock Stars. The first part of the day was spent shooting at Thee Parkside – a bar and indie rock venue in

Using a clap board when shooting with multiple cameras like we did for *Fixed Gears Fast Girls* helps editors in synching up sound and footage.

San Francisco's Potrero Hill, where I directed two queer sex scenes, one between myself and Dia Zerva on top of the bar, and another between Dylan Ryan and Dia Zerva in the very punk-rock bathroom of the venue. I only had a budget for our videographer to shoot with us for one day, and I still had another scene to shoot at an apartment I was renting on the other side of town.

For this final scene, I'd be performing with my real-life partner, James Mogul. We set up pretty quickly and thought it would be no problem. We shot the narrative intro and then went into the blowjob. Unfortunately, as does happen with many mortal men, my dear love had a challenge in maintaining an erection. It became clear, as we were nearing the time that our videographer had to leave, that I would need to think of another solution. I had a second camera on set for behind-the-scenes, and I suggested that while I was sucking on my partner's cock, we get a shot of James reaching for that camera, then a shot of him pointing the camera at me while I was sucking his cock. After we got that shot I was able to let our videographer go home. The following day, with my behind-the-scenes camera, we were able to resume the scene, this time with James holding the camera and shooting the completion of the scene from his point of view, with only the two of us in the room. In the edit, the change in the look of the footage made sense because we saw James pick up the camera and understood that we were now gazing at the action through his lens.

I'm often very close to my subjects without being in their way. Developing that comfort, trust and dialogue with your performers in all of your pre-production is key to developing this shared space between the camera and the performers. Always be aware of the performers' comfort, and any tensions you might find in their bodies. Communicate to your performers that if in any way you are too close or in their way, that they can call "Hold," and ask for space. The comfort of your performers and giving them the space they need is key in holding space for the scene while documenting their sexual expression.

While shooting, try to avoid a "floating camera," unless it is used sparingly and with great intent. What I mean by floating camera is allowing the camera to constantly be panning up and down the action. This is distracting and can make viewers feel seasick. It's fine to include a succinct pan into a shot, but it shouldn't be shaky, or be used as a technique for shooting an entire scene.

Speaking of avoiding shaky camera footage, I highly recommend a tripod or monopod. I don't always use them, but they are helpful in preventing your camera from shaking. Especially with small cameras, having some type of stabilizer can be really helpful. Personally I'm not a huge gear-head, but there is a lot of gear out there that can really help with this. You can also get really crafty and create DIY videocamera dollies.

If I know that I might be a little shaky with my camera footage then I make it part of my film. For example, my very successful series *A Woman's POV* was all about handing the camera to women while they were having sex. I had a primary camera that would shoot over the shoulder of one of the women, and then a second camera that the women would hand back and forth throughout the scene. The trembling camera was being held by a woman who was orgasming, whose gaze was on another woman who was smiling up into the trembling camera while her hand fucked the camera-holder, which really accentuated the emotional impact of the viewers' experience rather than detracting from it. Some of the footage is definitely shaky, but the viewer understands that the camera is an extension of the performer, and feels like they are intimately a part of the scene.

Other films that I've directed, such as *The Real L Word: San Francisco*, are presented as "mockumentaries," and the videographer is acknowledged as a character. In this case, some camera movement is less distracting than a narrative in which the videographer and camera are not acknowledged during the film. We see examples of this in mainstream television mockumentary series such as the *The Office* and *Modern Family*.

LIGHTING

I like to work with natural light. If I'm working in a house or studio with little to no natural light, I consider it essential to have

At my Erotic Film School where I teach, we use additional lights due to the location being indoors without a lot of natural light.

a videographer with a full light kit – or a videographer and a gaffer. The gaffer is the videographer's right-hand person, who rigs all the lights. For some films this is going to be more important than others. If you are interested in doing your own lighting, I highly recommend practicing a great deal before being on set, and allowing at minimum an hour for setting up lighting. Bad lighting or bad sound can make a fabulous film totally unappealing.

I am not a master of lighting. I know this, and it's important to know your strengths and weaknesses. So if I need a pro for lighting, I bring one in. For films like *The Curse of Macbeth,* which I shot in a warehouse with no windows, it was key for me to have a great videographer and gaffer to pull off the post-apocalyptic Shakespearean look I was going for.

I like to work with natural and available light. I love to shoot outside, and in locations with big windows where lots of beautiful light can spill in. If you are shooting in a house with dark paint and dark colors on the wall, you will notice your light gets swallowed up. Brighter and lighter colors will allow the light to reflect.

Two of my favorite rooms in the house to shoot in are the kitchen and bathroom. Generally these rooms tend to be light and bright, and even minimal natural light really reflects off of the tile that we often find in bathrooms and kitchens.

Shooting Isis Love and Niki Darling for *Lesbians in the Wild,* out in our urban jungle of Golden Gate Park.

If you're using natural light, remember to start early in the morning. You can't really explain to the sun that your performers are running late and you need it to set an hour later on your production day. The sun will do its thing and it doesn't pull overtime – so start early, daylight is a-burnin'!

One of my films, *Lesbians in the Wild*, was completely shot outside, and I scheduled all four scenes for outside on the same day. We had to scout each shoot location, then meet with the next two performers. The final scene ended up being shot completely in the dark, outside in the woods. The sun slipped right through our fingers, but we ended up lighting the scene with flashlights and making it this kind of creepy, arty, sexy scene in the dark. If you're working with natural light, remember not to overcommit or overbook your day of shooting, and always be prepared to come up with a Plan B.

There are small lights you can purchase that affix to your camera; these can come in handy for a C-Light. A C-light is your close-up light for close-up penetration shots. If your film involves shooting close-ups of penetration (it doesn't have to – its totally up to you – you make up the rules), often penetration can become shadowed and difficult to see, so a close-up light can assist in lighting the shot.

You might have have heard the term "opening up for the camera": Whether you need or want this for your film depends on your film, your mission and what you are aiming to shoot. I personally prefer very open sex positions and find them more enjoyable, but finding positions that are super hot and comfortable for your performers always takes priority.

AUDIO

I won't be saying a lot about audio. Some filmmakers will find this aspect more important than I do. Some directors will have bigger mics attached to their cameras, either with or without a windsock. Some directors will have a boom mic and a boom operator. A boom mic is a mic that is held up above the subjects to pick up their audio. The boom operator holds the mic above the action, but out of the camera's frame. The boom operator is listening to the audio coming in through earphones, to ensure that the audio is recording clearly and beautifully. There are also small mics that can attach to clothing, which might be affixed during something like an interview.

For the most part, unless it is something that my videographer and team are already set up with and proficient at using, and that I believe could actually advance the quality of my film in some way, I simply don't use any of these audio technologies. I use whatever mic is on my camera and that's it. If I'm shooting outside a windsock can be helpful, especially in the breezy Bay Area where I do most of my shooting. I'm not saying you shouldn't do it, or that I won't one day experiment with some different audio technologies, but thus far I haven't found it necessary to invest in separate audio mics. That said, some of my past videographers have at times used separate mics – but unless they were completely well-versed in the equipment, I opted not to use them. I'd rather have us using equipment that we are comfortable and masterful with, than experiencing botched audio along our learning curve.

Something we do always want to be mindful around regarding audio is turning off all cell phones on set. Don't set them to "vibrate," set them to "off." You don't want a cell phone going off to ruin your orgasm shot. Similarly, don't have music on while you're shooting, and don't keep heaters or air conditioners on – they are loud. You might not notice this sort of ambient sound as your ears adjust, but on film the heaters and air conditioners can be incredibly loud. This might mean if it is summer and hot, that you have to stop frequently for breaks to turn the air back on and cool things down.

Listen around you. Are there any buzzing lights? Turn off the fridge and freezer if you are shooting anywhere near the kitchen; these appliances make a detectable buzzing. Be sure to record one minute of room tone prior to shooting, in case you need the audio of ambient room tone for the edit. While doing so, make sure everyone on set is completely quiet while you say, "Room tone," then let the camera roll for one minute, recording only audio.

PHOTOS

There are a few different types of photos you might want to shoot on your film. Prior to shooting the sex scenes, you will want to shoot solo shots of each performer. These act as great profile photographs for your performers, and are a way for performers to warm up in front of the camera. In mainstream porn we call these "pretty girl" photographs, and they are generally first shot in an outfit, then taking off articles of clothing in a slow strip tease, into lingerie, and finally solo nude photographs. I aim to shoot around fifty fully clothed shots, fifty in lingerie and fifty nude. This is simply a template, and may or may not be helpful for you. Take what works for you – queer it up and make it your own.

Many of the performers I shoot are genderqueer or trans, and my version of "pretty girl" photographs are more "sexual portraits." Remember, it's not about fitting your performers into a mold or formula, but about how to honor and celebrate them as the individuals that they are. What clothes do they feel really sexy in? Maybe it's a black leather vest or their binder and a strap-on, or boxer shorts. I think some of the most beautiful photos taken of me were these black and white shots of me wearing my girlfriend's black sports bra and boxer shorts. I felt totally celebrated in my gender and sexuality, exactly as I was, without expectation of being more or different. I try to hold that space for my performers as well.

Sometimes having your performer pick some music that they like can help them to relax in front of the camera. In these photos you really want to create space and capture your performer enjoying themselves, their body and who they are, while making a connection with the camera. This is a time for them to shine in an outward expression of their personality. These clothed shots can make for great promo shots on social media, or platforms that require more coverage of the body.

After solo shots we typically shoot what in mainstream porn is referred to as the "prom shots." The prom shots are clothed and partially clothed photographs of the performers coupled together in an affectionate way, embracing and facing their bodies out toward the camera, in a way that mimics a very sexy prom photo. In these shots, we are looking for connection between the performers and between the performers and the camera. This can often be achieved with eye contact, if one of the performers is looking at the camera and the other performer is looking at the person who's embracing them.

After the prom photos, which also can make excellent clothed promotional shots, then we traditionally move into the sex photo stills. These can be a great way for the performers to block out the positions and toys that they may want to use during their scene on-set. This also allows the still photographer to be finished and out of the way while the video is being shot, and avoids camera clicks turning up in the audio of your film.

13 CUT & PASTE: THE BARE BONES OF EDITING

◆

YOU REMEMBER THAT SHOT LIST YOU COMPOSED earlier in the book? Okay, dig that out. You remember when you were holding the camera and shooting all those specific shots that you listed on your shot list, and then when you moved into shooting the sex scene you captured thirty seconds of close-up footage and then thirty seconds of a wide shot? Well, now you are going to go through the footage that you shot and find those pictures, those shots.

You can assemble them according to your shot list, or get creative and play around with the sequence. The way in which you assemble these shots can create different emotional responses for your viewer.

Watch some of your favorite films and see how the tempo of the cuts or the sequence of the narrative affects you emotionally. You can use the same images to tell very different stories, based on sequence, tempo, the shots you decide to keep in or cut out, and the audio that you use or don't use.

I am not a master of editing, but I have spent hundreds of hours behind a computer screen-editing footage. I learned how to edit the same way I learned most of my filmmaking skills – by doing it. Some people totally geek out on editing and absolutely love it. I wouldn't say that I love it, but once I'm in the midst of editing a project I truly enjoy it. I find it radically gratifying to sculpt a project from the footage that I've shot and really see my project blossom into a realized vision.

Sometimes, while I'm editing a film, imagery or ideas will come to mind that make the film even more amazing. Or I'll notice that my videographer wasn't really able to get the solid shot I was hoping for during a certain bit of dialogue, and have to think of another way to accomplish my vision. In my most recently released film, *Tangled Heart Strings*, a queer erotic mockumentary about a femme, a rocker and a guitar, there was a scene in which the poly-triad goes to a woo-woo rocker sex coach (played by me), Goddess Arboreal. Goddess Arboreal is a totally surreal character who is trying to get the triad to release their emotions "like wild ponies." She goes further into the metaphor of the ponies and setting your emotions free, encouraging the triad to "wiggle their pony ears" and "set their pony hooves galloping through the meadow." Goddess Arboreal chants her words, so often I overlaid audio of her voice chanting "om," allowing the audio to reverberate through the characters and the viewer in a surreal experience. I found vintage 1950s stock footage of ponies running through a meadow that was quickly spliced throughout Goddess Arboreal's surreal pony monologue. What resulted was absurdist magic. It was exactly what I was going for, and something that I became inspired by once I was in the thick of the edit.

It can help to remember that your audio and visual tracks are separate media. For example, if there is audio that came out beautifully, and the sound bite is great but the performer is out of focus or the shot was shaky, you can grab and splice the audio and set it to another image – either overlaying it onto an image of your performers that compliments the audio, or finding free stock footage,

Working hard at editing *The StarrLust Experience.*

or shooting something more abstract to compliment the sound bite. Remember to think outside of the box.

Feeling out the energy of a film or a scene, seeing how it feels and what is being conveyed emotionally, is one of the things I stay mindful of while editing. If it feels like the scene is dragging and that's not what you were hoping for, take notice of that. You might have excess dialogue that you don't need, and will want to edit some of it to move the film along.

Another major component of editing that affects the emotional response of the viewer is audio. Does your project have music set to it? If so, what emotion are you trying to convey, and what type of music do you need? Local indie bands or college musicians are a great source for film music. It's a great way for the musicians to get exposure; you can pay them a small fee and dramatically infuse your film with another layer of depth and emotion. Reach out to some of the indie bands you know or meet and are impressed with at small venues and local bars and clubs. Let them know about your film and your vision, and explain that you feel their music might be a good fit for your film.

My husband, James Mogul, who is also a filmmaker, once asked a violinist that he met in a subway station if he could record his music for an erotic film he was working on for his rope bondage website, Nawashibari.com. He paid the musician, recorded his music onto a computer, and had him sign a music release (make sure to have your musicians sign a release – agreements are made to keep friends). The music sounded beautiful in the film.

I've also paid to have folks compose music for scenes in my films. It was really fun to show them scenes or describe the mood, pacing and influences behind the scene and have someone compose music to fit. Music and audio are elements that can either really help or hurt a film, so finding the right music and audio for your film is important.

Sometimes I edit my own films. Other times I hand a feature film over to a professional editor to polish up a rough cut that I have done, to add any fancy features and to handle titles, credits, and any problems I might have run into that I don't know how to fix.

Editing can feel like a game of Tetris: each block or shot has a home and needs to be placed there. It's a time-consuming art form that takes immense focus. I highly recommend that when you feel you have lost your focus, and you're tired, and your eyes are having a difficult time staring at the screen, that you save your film and continue the next day. In fact, save your film and your edit as often as possible. There is nothing worse than working for hours on an edit only to have your computer crash and lose all the work that you have been doing.

Learning to edit improved my filmmaking exponentially. I got better at capturing the shots and footage on-set that I really wanted in the final edit.

There are many types of editing software. Many filmmakers have been switching to the new Adobe Premier, but I still enjoy editing on my Final Cut Pro 7. Some people find free editing software online or from a friend. Some of the free software might be a bit more clunky, but for the most part, if you learn how to edit on one program it won't be a steep learning curve when switching to another.

You load the footage you shot into the machine that you are editing on. For most cameras being sold today, you will be recording onto an SD card. Some computers have an SD card reader, or you can buy an external SD card reader that plugs into the USB slot on your computer. Once you insert the SD card, it should appear on your computer's desktop. You want to create a file for your film footage on your computer and drag the footage, the movie files, into that folder.

The first thing I do with my footage is watch it. I go through each file and watch each movie clip in the folder. If it's a shaky clip or "accidental footage," test footage, etc., I delete it. If it's footage I don't need for this project, I don't want it in the folder. I remove it so I can more easily organize the footage that I do need.

If there are multiple scenes to the film, organize the footage into folders by scene, or by who is in the scene. Then you can find the footage you want when you need it. Once your footage is organized, you can open up your editing program, start a new project, name it, save it and upload footage for your first scene.

A timeline toward the bottom of the screen has a number of rows for video and audio. There will also be a "viewer" and a "canvas." When you click on one of the clips that you uploaded to the editing program, it will open in the canvas.

You should have your shot list out, and know whether you're starting with the first shot on your original list. Find the start of your shot in the open clip – play the clip and pause it where you want the shot to start by pressing the space bar. Now press down the command button and "i" (for in). A marker should appear on your canvas that shows the clip. The marker is indicating the "in," or start point of your shot. Now press the space bar and allow the clip to play to where you see the shot ending. When you find the end point of the shot, press the space bar again to pause the film. Now press command-o (for out) and another marker should appear on the canvas, indicating the end of the shot you've cut out of the clip.

Now take your mouse and drag the cut edit of the shot to the very beginning of your timeline. Press command-s to save your first edit. Congratulations, you're editing!

Whatever is on the timeline should appear in the "viewer" box, so you can now view the edit that you did in the viewer, as long as you move your mouse to the beginning of your timeline. Well, how does it look? Is your first shot as you envisioned it would be? Move on to your second shot, third shot and so on, all the way down the film. It's essentially a cut-and-paste of pictures.

There are entire books on video editing, and hundreds of editing tutorials on sites like Youtube – so if you get stumped, which we all do along the way, don't be afraid to do a little research. I have run into so many tech glitches and incompatibility issues over the years, but you are never the first one to experience an issue. Google it, and usually there is an entire forum dedicated to your issue, and someone will have found a solution. You can also utilize social media to see if someone else has run into a similar issue with their editing software, or you can have another editor help you or consult with you when you run into problems.

14 DISTRIBUTION: HOW TO GET YOUR FILM INTO THE WORLD

YOU NOW HAVE A FINISHED FILM. IT'S WHAT you dreamt about, and it's all cut together in a beautiful package. Now to send that package out into the world.

When you first envisioned this film, where did you envision it screening? Who did you envision watching the film? In this chapter we are going to explore some potential destinations for your film so you can create your dream itinerary, and discover whether it's possible for you to make a living as a DIY pornographer.

I was recently speaking at an event in Sydney, Australia, "Intimate Conversation with Madison Young," where folks were given room to ask the intimate questions that they were most curious about. I delivered a long monologue on the difference between mainstream and feminist pornography, a key difference resting on the fact that the sole focus of mainstream pornography is to generate profit, while DIY and feminist pornography stem from feminist and

Discussing feminist porn with Gala Vanting in Sydney, Australia, while screening clips of my films like *Art House Sluts* and *Tangled Heart Strings.*

sex-positive ethos, and are presented as part of a political, social and cinematic movement to create change in the way that we think about and discuss sex, gender, desire and sexuality. When I finished, the first question was, "So is it possible to make money as a DIY and feminist pornographer?"

Of course. Is it enough to make a living from? It depends on where you live, and dozens of other factors. What I do know is that it is not easy to make money as a DIY pornographer. For me, DIY pornography is one of many aspects of my artistic practice. There are many ways to generate funds for your DIY porn, and even to make a career out of creating DIY porn, with DIY porn being part of your filmmaking career or your career as an artist or sexual educator.

I get a lot of letters from women who tell me that they want to start a career as a feminist or queer porn performer. This is a more challenging proposition. Not because it is challenging to perform in feminist or queer porn, but because there are still so few queer porn companies that to base a career on performing for the few that currently shoot on a regular basis would not result in a livable income – unless a performer also produces their own films, or owns the content and can make money on the films they performed in for years to come. This is actually the route that I suggest.

As a performer, if you take control of your own stories and images by not only performing, but directing and producing your own films, you now gain a great deal more control over your voice, your brand, your story and your ability to make a career and sustainable income.

Of course this does require a great deal more time and commitment to establish a consistent income. I not only make films on a regular basis, but I write about DIY and feminist erotic filmmaking, teach erotic filmmaking, speak and give lectures and presentations on erotic filmmaking, present at live events and screenings of my films, and work on distribution for the films that feel most exciting to me. Remember the form of distribution you decide on doesn't have to be just one of the distribution methods that I mention below, but can encompass them all, or just the ones you are truly excited to be a part of.

Or you can create totally new avenues of distribution for your film! Discover new and exciting ways to get art and media out into the world and don't be afraid to try something new. Wanna distribute your new short erotic film about a riot grrrl as an insert in a zine that you made to accompany the film? Go for it! Wanna bundle the sound track for the film and the film together to reach out to music and erotic film lovers? Go for it! I was always impressed with the Vivid Alt soundtracks and the way they integrated music and sex in their films to really document the sexual culture and stories of punk, indie and alt cultures. Their work was executed beautifully and I highly recommend you checking it out. They no longer create new work, but they have a huge canon of awesome films to check out for inspiration, that includes directors like Kimberly Kane, Dana Dearmond, Eon McKai and Dave Naz.

I have heard from naysayers that in the decline of the porn economy, it is nearly impossible to make a living as a DIY pornographer, but I don't agree. I do agree that the economy and technology have changed pretty rapidly since I started directing a decade ago, and that traditional modes of "porn marketing" just don't work in the same way that they did before the market became so saturated with content. But if we create something that stands as a unique, individual erotic film with a strong vision and values, and if we honor that individual film, the participants and our process, we can make a living through our artistry.

I think the idea of a declining porn economy is coming from a place of examining the current structure in which mainstream porn is sold. The structure of mainstream porn is failing mainstream porn; why would it work for us? And why would we think that the only way to reach our audience is through the same avenues that mainstream porn uses? To make a living in the field of DIY pornography you must be innovative, think outside the box, not be afraid of trying something new, be resourceful, dedicated, passionate, and not afraid to fearlessly pursue what you believe in.

METHODS OF DISTRIBUTION

Film Festivals. An exciting type of venue that has blossomed over the last decade is erotic film festivals and screenings specifically focused on erotic film. These occur throughout the States, South America, Asia, Europe and Australia. Some of the film festivals are touring festivals, like the Bike Smut Film Festival and the HUMP Festival. Other film festivals are annual or one-time events that are organized by kink, queer, sex-positive and/or feminist communities. Many of these festivals are grass-roots efforts and are largely volunteer-run.

It's very rare that a festival is able to fly in a filmmaker, but if you're able to travel to the festival it is always an incredible and nerve-wracking experience to watch your film on the big screen. This is also an remarkable experience in terms of meeting other filmmakers and distributors, and representatives from erotic film channels, web sites, VOD sites, producers and more.

Since I also perform in many of my films, I've also had the indescribable pleasure of seeing my vulva huge on a big screen in front of several hundred other people in a dark theater. To see people sitting together and witnessing sexual pleasure in a public setting is empowering. Many of the festivals include other events such as workshops, lectures, Q&A and filmmaker speaking engagements. These events present you with an opportunity to really speak about your film in a theater with other people who appreciate erotic filmmaking.

I've included a list of erotic film festivals for you to check out. This list is always changing and growing, so make sure to do your own research online. If you are making queer DIY porn, reach out to queer and LGBT film festivals as well. Does your city have an annual art house film festival or avant-garde film festival, and you're making art house porn? Don't be afraid to propose new programming for your local festivals, with suggestions for other filmmakers who are creating work similar to yours. Mark on your calendar the submission dates and start sending your films in. You can do it!

Successful models of erotic film festivals:

Cinekink (New York, San Francisco, LA, Las Vegas and other locations)	www.cinekink.com
The Berlin Porn Film Festival (Berlin)	www.pornfilmfestivalberlin.de
Hump! by Dan Savage (Touring festival based out of Seattle)	www.humpseattle.com
Hard Liquor and Porn Festival (Montreal, London and Sydney)	www.hardliquorandporn.com

Perv Queerotic Film Festival (Sydney)	www.pervfilmfestival.com
Painted Lips and Lolly Licks Festival (Ottowa, Canada)	www.mayfairtheatre.ca
East Bay Express Briefs (Oakland, CA)	www.eastbayexpress.com
Pornotopia (Albuquerque, NM)	www.selfservetoys.com
La Fête du Slip Sex Positive Porn Festival (Switzerland)	www.lafeteduslip.ch
Porny Days Film Festival (Zurich)	www.pornydays.ch
Forbidden Film Fest (Austin, TX)	www.forbiddenfilmfest.com
Muestra Marrana Festival (Spain)	www.muestramarrana.org
Fetisch Film Festival (Kiel, Germany)	www.traumgmbh-kiel.de
Bike Smut (Touring Festival)	www.bikesmut.com
New York City Porn Film Festival (New York)	www.nycpornfilmfestival.com
CatalystCon (Los Angeles, CA)	www.catalystcon.com
Seattle Erotic Art Festival (Seattle, WA)	www.seattleerotic.org

Membership Site. Maybe you're interested in offering scenes from your films, as well as photography and essays, on a membership site. With a membership site, there is an expectation that the site will be dynamic and updated regularly. For some sites that can only shoot one scene per month, one week's update might be photos from the scene, the next week is the behind-the-scenes video interview about the scene, the following week is the video of the scene, and the fourth week is a post-scene interview. With a membership site, you would set up a paying structure through a company such as Verotel or CCBill. There are some initial set-up costs, though, and setting up such a site can be a great deal of maintenance, take quite a bit of work, and require a solid team with a lot of energy. So just be prepared. After you have four scenes you could create a compilation DVD of the scenes, and still submit your scenes as short films at Erotic Film Festivals if you chose to.

Successful examples of membership sites (all Feminist Porn Award nominees) are:

- www.makelovenotporn.tv
- www.liandradahl.com
- www.IshotMyself.com
- www.CrashPadSeries.com
- www.TheArtofBlowjob.com
- www.brightdesire.com
- www.ifeelmyself.com
- www.juicypinkbox.com
- www.naughtynatural.com
- www.the-female-orgasm.com
- www.welovegoodsex.com
- www.wendysummers.com
- www.wendywilliamsxxx.com
- www.xconfessions.com
- www.JizLee.com
- www.LilyCade.com
- www.DaneJones.com
- www.PaddedKink.com | Kelly Shibari
- www.HeavenlySpire.com | Shine Louise Houston

Some membership sites also buy scenes for their own sites, such as MakeLoveNotPorn.tv, IshotMyself.com, BeautifulAgony.com, GoodDykePorn.com and others.

DVD. You can always put your film on DVD and have it sold at sex-positive stores, your website, and any events, festivals or conferences you might be speaking at in conjunction with the film. Be mindful that DVDs as a medium are largely disappearing: DVD sales have gone dramatically down in the last seven years. I used to do large-scale replication of films, but these days I try to do smaller DVD duplication runs. I find that the majority of my DVDs sell at live events where event-goers are interested in purchasing something physical and getting a DVD signed.

One alternative I have started is creating limited edition DVDs as art pieces, such as my Anus Print original art-covered DVDs for *The StarrLust Experience.* This is a collectible art piece, as well as media which folks can watch. It has a higher price point, but can even be framed and hung as artwork afterward.

As a director, I've adapted to changing technology and individuals' preferences as to the media format in which they watch erotic film. One way in which I've accomplished this is by selling collections of my work on USB drives, so folks that are interested in receiving something physical can acquire an entire collection of films in a digital format.

VOD. VOD stands for Video on Demand. This is largely how folks are replacing the DVD. VOD is an iTunes or Amazon-like format for erotic media, in which the buyer can purchase a film and stream that individual film from their computer. You can offer VOD on your own website, and also send your film to other VOD streaming sites that support indie and feminist erotic films. Check out other VOD platforms' submission process. Making your films available on multiple VOD platforms widens and diversifies your viewing audience, and creates multiple monthly income streams from a single film.

Some successful examples of VOD sites to check out are:

- www.PinkLabel.tv
- www.HotMoviesforHer.com
- www.HotMovies.com

- www.AEBN.net
- www.KinkOnDemand.com
- www.Clips4Sale.com
- www.LustCinema.com

Live Shoots. Offering live content or live access to the filming process can be a fun way to get folks excited about your film before it is even released. You can also sell online tickets on sites like EventBrite for folks to access behind-the-scenes online streaming of your live shoot. You can broadcast your live shoot on platforms like Ustream.com, and send your event's private URL to all the ticket buyers. It's best to have one person on set handling all the live tech elements, so that you as a director can focus on your directorial responsibilities.

Some successful examples of live shoots to check out are:

- www.TheUpperFloor.com
- www.NinaHartley.com

Art Galleries. Maybe your erotic film is more appropriate for an art gallery, or installed as a video art installation. Thinking and presenting our work outside the box is one of the strengths of DIY porn. We are creating new ways for people to view sex; we have something to say about sex, and we are not churning out a product that we are attempting to mass market. Instead, each film, each project can be as individual as you are. In a video installation created by artist Jonathan Harris titled "I Love Your Work," the artist created an interactive documentary about the private lives of nine women who make lesbian porn. The video piece consisted of more than two thousand ten-second video clips, taken at five-minute intervals over ten consecutive days, totaling around six hours of footage. The video installation exhibited at the Sundance Film Festival in 2014 and featured Dylan Ryan, Ryan Keely, Ela Darling and Jincey Lumpkin.

Some galleries and art festivals that have exhibited video works on the topic of sexuality include:

- www.SeattleErotic.org (Seattle, WA)
- www.RochestEroticArtFest.org (Rochester, NY)
- www.ArtUndressed.com (Miami, FL)

Your Own Dirty Movie Club or Porn Night. Do you want to reach out to your local community or take distribution and screening into your own hands? Interested in cultivating a DIY porn-watching community where you currently can't find one? Start your own Dirty Movie Club or Porn Screening Night! Whether it's at a bar, club, indie theater or on someone's rooftop, don't be afraid to make your own thing happen. Wouldn't a Dirty Movie Club out in a cornfield in the middle of nowhere be extraordinary? Perhaps in a community garden? I once screened an evening of all queer eco-sexual outdoor sex scenes in a garden in San Francisco, and it was a magical evening. The world is your canvas – don't be afraid to ask and discover your allies.

Along the way, you will also discover people who will not be supportive of erotic film, DIY porn or outward displays of sexuality. You are entering into a realm that embraces and celebrates a part of our humanity that is still steeped in shame. Your work is brave and it might frighten some people. Your events might get shut down. You might encounter problems with venues or disgruntled parents or the police. Have a plan. Know your rights, and know that the work you are doing is important. Have a lawyer. Have legal support and allies, and follow your heart; lead with compassion.

Cable TV and International Markets. Even DIY porn can find itself on cable TV, both within and outside the United States. It's another exciting way to get your films out into the world, and is another revenue stream for your DIY porn-making career.

Some successful examples of cable tv to check out are:

- Pure Play Broadcasting (www.pureplaybroadcasting.com)
- French Lover (FrenchLover.tv)
- DuskTV (2GrapesMedia.com)

My production assistant scouted out this amazing location by the Sutro Baths in San Francisco. The vibrant graffiti and ocean landscape were perfect for this ecosexual mermaid/sailor scene performed by Beretta James and Lorelei Lee.

15 MARKETING AND PROMOTION: CONNECTING WITH YOUR AUDIENCE

MARKETING. FOR SOME OF US THAT WORD FEELS dirty and uncomfortable, conjuring visions of pushy salespeople, porno spam, overt pop-ups and ads that try to convince us that we need their product through psychological manipulation of images, playing on our insecurities. Many advertisements are "smart ads," playing only to their key demographics, based on our social media profiles. These provide marketers with exactly the information they need to figure out who we are, and what we are most likely to purchase, so they can shove it down our throats. Yeah, so I'm not a huge fan of the advertising industry, as you can probably tell.

One of the reasons I make feminist DIY pornography is that its roots and values lie, not in playing into the commercial structure of mainstream pornography, but in creating porn based on feminist ethos, artistic merit and a celebration of the individual. So once I became a feminist pornographer who created films, I had to figure out a way to connect those films with an audience, with communities, with individuals. In the same way that DIY pornographers had to create new ways of documenting sexual culture and creating films that explored the depths of sexual desire, we had to create new ways to let people know about our films.

As someone who not only creates erotic film, but also coordinates and curates art-focused events on a regular basis, I am familiar with community organizing and getting the word out about my work, in fun, DIY, guerrilla-marketing styles that work for my brand.

So how do you figure out what is right for your brand, or even what your brand is? Remember the vision statement and mission statement that you developed at the very beginning of the book? The one based on who you are, what you believe in, and the impact you hope to make in the world through your filmmaking? Find it. In fact, I hope you've been referencing it and using it as a guide throughout this filmmaking process.

That vision and those values should inform your brand and your films. The reason they inform your marketing and your films is that they are what you are passionate about, what you believe in, why you are making film. These values are the most important things to communicate to people when marketing your films. They're what your audience will remember the most about your work.

People have asked me how I have managed to create such a cohesive brand for my work and my career through out the years, and I was actually a little surprised. I hadn't spent much time actually thinking about branding, but I was always focused on my vision, my passion and my values, with a clear concept of the impact that I hoped to create. In following these markers, I was able to develop a cohesive brand that was authentic to who I am. The vision, the values and the passion come first, the authentic branding is informed directly by the concise communication of these ingredients.

WHO IS YOUR AUDIENCE?

One of the most common things you will read in marketing books is this question: Who is your audience? What is your demographic? It's something that everyone wants to know. Who is going to be buying your film (or is it even for sale)? Who is attending the events that you coordinate around your film productions – like film screenings, or art shows of photography from the film?

I've never really liked this question. It's another one of those things that makes me uncomfortable, because it lumps people into boxes rather than honoring the individual. And I'd rather make impacts in the lives of individual folks. However, I have found that there are certain commonalities amongst many of the individuals who attend my events and buy my films, and that has to do with how I choose to interact with the communities I'm a part of.

So this is what I've discovered about my audience: My porn-going, porn-watching, porn-buying, porn-talking audience tends to be other feminists, queers, sex workers, kink community, kink-curious, porn-curious, parents out on date nights, young college students, women and gender studies majors in college, straight guys who watch a lot of porn and stumble upon my work and are intrigued, couples who like to watch porn together, feminist submissives, and folks who have grown up in conservative environments where they were unable to outwardly celebrate or explore their sexuality. I have had the joy of hearing so many unique stories, both online and out in the world at events. These are the commonalities that I hear, that I see in the stories from those that resonate with my work. It's a wide demographic, though sometimes it's narrower because of the event I'm doing, the specific focus of a film, or the venue. But knowing the individuals who are excited about my work tells me what venues to present my work at, and where to promote my screenings, appearances or premieres.

I know to promote my film *Pregnant with Desire* at both baby and pregnancy conventions, conferences and stores, and my docu-porn film on my decade-long romance with my dominant, *To Sir with Love,* at our local leather shops, kink café, and BDSM dungeons and community events. I can pair up live events or talks on feminism and pornography, or feminism and submission. I can create panels on certain topics and then screen a clip from my film *To Sir with Love,* or *Women Reclaiming Sex on Film,* and offer the film for sale, and do a signing at the event.

These types of events, in which we bring in other voices, experts and fellow industry-professionals, present an opportunity for you, as well as other filmmakers or professionals, to further a conversation on sexuality and film with your community. Art and film can be a platform or diving board for these conversations. This strategy also helps you create allies and relationships with your fellow filmmakers.

Do you live in an area where there are simply no other "out" erotic filmmakers? You can bring in erotica writers, sex therapists or sex coaches, or work with your cast of performers and crew on presenting together. Also, in this great age of technology, you can Skype in other DIY porn performers and directors from around the globe. All it takes is a projector, a white wall and a computer with an Internet connection. If you approach many filmmakers online, either through their websites or social media, they are typically very willing to help and to participate in the conversation.

MOVIE POSTERS OR FLYERS

Movie posters and flyers are a great way to get creative with your film. Your poster might just be promoting the film, or it might be more specifically promoting a screening of your film, another film launch event, or even a movie tour!

Your poster can be as creative as you are. You can create an image and basic text, slogan and URL, and screen-print really compelling hand-printed posters that you can sell at the screening. I have watched an intern of mine mock up a flyer for one of my screenings on their smart phone! Did you know there is an app for that? You can also do an old-school cut-and-paste flyer, and Xerox a zillion copies to plaster the city with.

Screenings and Q&As like this one for *Tangled Heart Strings* allow the audience a chance to get excited and engage with the performers and filmmaker.

Wanna go with a more professional look? Find a local printer or a place like Kinkos, and you can print a couple of hundred glossy 4x6 or 5x7 club cards.

Sometimes you will run into a printer that won't print erotic material, but that has only happened to me once in the past decade. Also, your posters and flyers don't need to be explicit in any way. The text should state that the event is eighteen and over or twenty-one and over, depending on the venue. The images should be intriguing, but don't give everything away. Make it funny or smart, and create an image and poster that invites the viewer to engage further, to explore. Invite them into your world; make it a call to action.

PACKAGING

DIY porn gives us space to truly think outside the box, even when considering our box cover! For one of my recent films, *The StarrLust Experience,* which was an art-house film inspired by the David Bowie persona Ziggy Stardust, I decided to make the packaging of the film itself a piece of art. I knew I wanted to offer the DVD of the film as a limited run of only one hundred films. I sold each film at a premium price of $50, as opposed to the typical DVD that sells for somewhere between $20 to $30. The packaging was made by hand from original anus prints that I printed using archival ink, my anus, thick, white, watercolor paper that was affixed around DVD-sized envelopes (which I constructed from cardboard envelopes.. The packaging was more than just a sexy image on the DVD; it was abstract, original, signed and numbered artwork that said something about the film and about me as a filmmaker.

So get creative. You don't have to operate within the machine of the porn industry in order to create, package and distribute your film. Look at the art world, the indie film and music worlds, at the ways in which they have packaged their media. Look at your Vision and Values statement for inspiration. Think about ways that you can honor your film as the individual work of art that it is; operate outside of the box. Maybe you're more of a crafter, or you love screen-printing. Maybe you sew DVD cozies that are screen-printed with an image or text on the front. Maybe you want to offer your film only on a USB, or as a collection of short films on a USB stick. Think of clever ways you can package the USB stick in a bookmark with the name of your film on, it or a slogan, like "DIY Porn Rocks!" When you think outside the box, it allows for more opportunities to collaborate with other artists and makers and to add your unique branding and sense of self to your project. In expressing yourself fully in your project, you will be empowering you viewer to celebrate themselves fully in their lives.

FILM SCREENINGS

Film screenings are a great way to promote your film and to celebrate your DIY porn on the big screen. So where do you screen your film? Is there an independent theater that screens more obscure and indie films in your city or town? Is there a theater, art gallery, bar, club or warehouse that hosts DIY, queer, kink or more counterculture focused events? Do some research and have a talk with the owner or events coordinator about venue rental, or hosting an event at their venue. Make sure to have your vision statement and values statement handy. Be able to speak passionately about your vision and give a short description of the film itself and the impact you expect it to have.

They also might be curious as to how many people you might expect for the event. This can be hard to estimate and really depends on the promotion of the event by both you and your cast and crew. When you and your cast and crew are whole-heartedly promoting the event with a six- to eight-week lead time, you can generally expect a fairly strong turnout.

Let's say you have ten people between the cast and crew who were involved in making the film, everyone in the film is local, and they're all really down with your vision and passionate about promoting the film. Then you can figure that probably each of those ten people will pull in at least five people to attend the film screening, so that would be fifty people even if no one else comes from the general public. It's important to think about your audience and try not to book the screening on a night on which there is a competing event.

One way to promote film screenings, and your film in general, is social media. Social media is not the only way to promote films or events, but it does expand your audience and can directly affect ticket sales.

Here is a basic rundown of some of the social media platforms that I've found helpful for DIY porn marketing, and how I use them.

Facebook. Some social media platforms are more porn-friendly/sex-friendly/body-friendly than others. Facebook is on the conservative end of that spectrum. Many of my friends have had accounts shut down or pages taken down, or have been censored or given warnings. Facebook has a "no nipples or genitalia" policy. I tend to speak on Facebook the way I would speak to my mom about my work. I make sure that the images that I post cover nipples and genitalia, and wouldn't draw attention for closer inspection. This is good to think about while you are in production: try to get some promotional shots of characters expressing emotion, connection and intimacy, without strictly relying on nudity.

Sometimes I use Facebook to put out calls for venues or crew or production assistants. It can also be a good space to post about your production process, the behind-the-scenes preparation of your production. It's helpful to create a separate page for your film or production company and have your cast and crew "Like" it. You can repost things from your page on your personal profile (if you can share your erotic filmmaking pursuits with all your FB friends).

Speaking of which, you should make sure to check your FB settings to see what level of privacy your profile is set for. Can everyone see your posts, or just your friends? You can also create a private group in which you could post regarding your erotic filmmaking. Decide what you're comfortable with, and what level of safety and privacy feel good to you.

I also use FB when I have events like screenings, premieres, panels or workshops pertaining to my filmmaking. Creating a FB event invitation lets folks know about your film event, casting calls or calls for interns or crew. Maybe you're looking for other artists working in the realm of sexuality to be on a panel with you. This is a great way to put a call out. Start exploring groups, and if you share with your network and let people know that it's okay for them to share with their networks or repost, soon word about your work and your film will be spreading throughout the Internet.

Twitter. Twitter has been extremely helpful in getting the word out about my films, and I see direct sales result from my Twitter posts. Twitter consists of quick, short messages. It can also become a dialogue in an open forum for others to read. The way Twitter operates is that folks post 140-character text statements that they publish to the world. It's similar to a Facebook update, but shorter. You send short broadcasts of media, photo, text or video out into the world,

This sexy and compelling promo photo for *Tangled Heart Strings* is even "Facebook safe."

and your photos and videos can be dirty! For the most part Twitter doesn't censor sexual content in the same way that Facebook does, so you can post more graphic content if you so choose, but I do also believe in not showing everything. You want to post enough to get folks really excited, and to buy their tickets to the premiere or event, or buy the film, but don't give the whole film away.

If you are just starting out with your company, you want to develop followers. Followers are the folks that will receive whatever you are posting. Often if you follow someone, they might follow you back. Also, if you broadcast that you have a Twitter account for your DIY porn on another social media platform on which you already have a following, or out to your email list, then people will follow you. Want folks to gain an interest in you and your film? Engaging in conversations or responding to colleagues within the feminist and DIY porn movements will gain you name recognition, and if folks enjoy what you are saying they will follow you as well.

People love photographs. Posting photos from events, behind-the-scenes, on-set or of film screenings or appearances gets a lot of reposts. You might be saying, okay, so I'm accumulating followers, what does that mean? It means your online audience is growing and they have an interest in your art and what you have to say. So share with them what you are creating and how they can be a part of it.

Are you looking for a marketing intern, are you casting for your next film, are you looking for a graphic designer or illustrator? Post about it and offer a direct link or email address where people can contact you. Offering a link to where they can apply or a contact email is key. This is also a key element to selling tickets to live screenings, appearances and events or selling copies of your film. It should take as few clicks as possible for people to buy your ticket, apply for an internship or buy your film. Too many clicks and you will lose your sale or the attention of your audience.

Instagram. Instagram is an application you can use directly from your phone, so if you have someone like an intern or assistant taking behind-the-scene photos on-set or at your event, they can be posting them directly to your Instagram account. Instagram is slightly more conservative, and I have received warnings for some of my behind-the-scenes shots, so we have started posting only Facebook-safe images to our Instagram account as well – clothed or at least covering nipples and genitals. You can also post photos of faces, hands, curling feet, entwined legs, reaction shots, etc. There are many creative shots you can come up with that tell the story and excite the viewer about your film and brand without showing nipples or genitals.

Tumblr. Tumblr is another anything-goes social media platform. There is plenty of porn on Tumblr. It's a blog-like platform that works for photos, video and text.

People who are into Tumblr are pretty die-hard about this platform. This is one of those millennial platforms that came in after I already had my groove going with Twitter and Facebook, and so I didn't really get into it so much. And that's okay. You don't have to be a pro at all these social media platforms, and if you choose not to, you don't have to interact with any of them. It's up to you to decide what feels good and authentic to you.

If you decide that social media isn't really your thing but that you still want a presence on these platforms, you can always find an intern or volunteer to help with your social media presence. If you choose to go that route, just be very clear with your team member as far as what your goals for your social media are, and be very clear about your needs, visions and values for your filmmaking practice and any specific films that you are working on. Communication, clear communication, is key.

Fetlife. Fetlife is primarily a kinky BDSM community forum with profiles. It's a social media site for kinksters. There are no limitations on posting images of nudity or sexual imagery. There are groups and forums, and this can be a great way to develop some dialogue and conversations with community about feminist and DIY porn, and promote your films and events. It is not a place for spam, so it's important to engage with individuals and groups in a way that is specific to your vision.

If you feel like your conversations and responses or posts are getting too cookie-cutter, take a deep breath and revisit the vision board that you created at the beginning of this book; revisit your vision statement and values. Close your eyes and daydream about your future film or your favorite moments of the film you have shot or directed. What inspired you in that process? What moments stood out as beautiful, "Aha!" moments?. Share those with your social media audience. Inspire others with your vision, your work and your experiences, and let them know how they can be a part of them.

Wordpress. Wordpress is a blogging platform that has easy-to-use, professional-looking themes, and an extremely user-friendly back end, allowing you to create simple websites with no prior knowledge of building a site or blog. I have used Wordpress to create sites for specific festivals, lecture series, films, books and artistic projects. It's an easy, quick and free way to have an online representation of your work. This can be a great place to announce pre-production, production, post-production, behind-the-scenes, and cast and crew appearances. It's an excellent place for your Vision and Values statement to live, as well as your contact information, a casting application, trailers for your films, and a way for people to pre-order or purchase your film or to buy tickets to your film-related events.

Once you have decided on a name for your erotic filmmaking company/collective/co-op, you can acquire a domain at a domain registrar like godaddy.com, and then redirect the URL to whatever your free Wordpress blog site is. Blog about the filmmakers and films that inspire you, your creative process, or images that evoke an emotion or hold interest for you as a filmmaker. Along with your email address, you can also list the ways in which folks can find you on social media, so that they can follow you there as well.

Trailers. A trailer for a film can be a great way to promote your project. It's nice to have a couple of different trailers. You can have a trailer for your film that is safe for Youtube and all social media outlets, with no nudity. This might contain exciting sexy music, text, a portion of the narrative and dialogue amongst the characters that makes us curious about them and their connection and flirtation with one another. Or you can reveal something really intriguing about them through their dialogue or action, followed by quick, short cuts of footage of the characters being intimate, but in which we don't see naked bodies. Perhaps instead we see a close shot of the characters making out, the grabbing of hair, eye contact, biting of a lip, two hands holding one another. You would be surprised how many incredibly hot shots you can find that don't contain the nude body.

Then you also want to have a trailer that contains some of the sex. Find footage that contains a lot of intensity, sexual tension, radically loving connection, drama or orgasm. You want to give the viewer an emotional feel for the roller coaster they are about to get onto, but just a peek. This trailer can go on your Wordpress blog, website or social media, and acts as a great vehicle for letting folks know about your film so they can pre-order or order the film from you.

If you are trying to raise funds for making your film, creating a non-nude trailer can be a smart way of having a single production day, just hiring your performers to do dialogue and clothed shots so that you have a trailer to use to promote the film, engage in fundraising efforts and pitch to distributors, press or producers.

Press Releases. A press release can be a great way to get the word out about your film, your screening or any of your film-related events. Start by having a press release template, and developing a press list of online news and media outlets, magazines, newspapers or anywhere else you might have an interest in broadcasting news about your filmmaking.

Make a list of magazines and media sites that you frequent. You can also research which media outlets post frequently about sex, erotic film, feminism or other topics that your film addresses. Gathering contacts for adult industry magazines and media outlets is also helpful. Two of the most notable of these are AVN Media and XBIZ.

You don't have to send press releases out to just industry magazines. Reflect back on who your community is, what your film represents, and consider media sources that also take an interest in those topics. Having non-explicit, non-nude promotional images to accompany your press release is a smart idea. Images help a journalist, writer or media outlet to visualize the story of your film or event. Here's a sample press release for you to consider what components might work for you, and to help you think about how you might model your own press release.

FOR IMMEDIATE RELEASE

MADISON YOUNG'S ARTGASM TO SCREEN THE EAST BAY PREMIERE OF EMILIE JOUVET'S *TOO MUCH PUSSY*

CONTACT: Madison Young, FEMINISTPORNNETWORK@GMAIL.COM

"ARTGASM: A MONTHLY EROTIC FILM NIGHT WHERE ARTIST VISION AND EROTIC MEDIA MEET IN CINEMATIC CLIMAX"
OAKLAND, CA – FRIDAY, MARCH 27TH, 2015
10:30 PM
THE NEW PARKWAY
474 24TH STREET
OAKLAND CA

Madison Young presents "ArtGasm: A Monthly Erotic Film Night," where artistic vision and erotic media meet in cinematic climax. Join us at the fabulous New Parkway Theater in Oakland every fourth Friday at 10:30pm, located at 474 24th Street, for food, community, beer, erotic and experimental films that are provocative, sexy and thought-provoking.

Come have a climactic ArtGasm with us as Madison Young hosts a series of engaging art-house erotic films from around the globe, and facilitates an audience Q&A with the filmmaker.

March 27th at 10:30pm, ArtGasm's second month of titillating films will feature an East Bay Premiere of Emilie Jouvet's award winning queer erotic "sex-positive road movie," *Too Much Pussy*. This brilliant and fierce feminist erotic film follows a troupe of erotic performance artists on a debauched European tour. They bring sexuality to the forefront, live and breathing, visceral and inescapable, right in front of your eyes. Jouvet further crosses the lines between porn, eroticism, art and activism with the live shows that challenge reserved notions.

Come see why Emilie Jouvet's *Too Much Pussy* won the Cliff Award at the Cannes Independent Film Festival.

Feminist Porn Network will be providing sexy goodie bags to the first fifty attendees, so buy tickets early and make sure to get to the theater to check out our selection of erotic art and films that will be on display and for sale at our Feminist Porn Network table.

Curator and Host Bio: Madison Young is a revolutionary feminist artist, activist, filmmaker, wordsmith and curator. Young's breadth of work in the realm of sexuality encompasses the documenting of our sexual culture in forty feature-length feminist pornographic films that have won numerous accolades, including six Feminist Porn Awards as well as numerous XBIZ and AVN nominations, and have been screened internationally. Young speaks on the topics of feminist pornography, feminism & sexuality and kink at universities including Yale University, Harvard University, Hampshire College, Northwestern University and UC Berkeley. Her writings have been published in the

Feminist Porn Studies Academic Journal as well as her recently released memoir, *Daddy*. She is currently writing *The DIY Porn Handbook: Documenting Our Sexual Revolution.*

Filmmaker Bios: Emilie Jouvet is a Graduate of the Beaux Arts and the Ecole Nationale Supérieure de la Photographie. She is a film director and photographer. Jouvet has been exploring the European queer scene for over fifteen years, her photographic work encompassing intimate portraits and subversive mise-en-scène. Her work has been shown all over Europe (Agnès B Gallery; the Maison Européenne de la Photographie, Paris; the Arles Photography Festival; Tristesse de Luxe Gallery, Berlin; ArtRebels Gallery, Copenhagen; and also San Francisco in 2010 and Tokyo in 2012).

In 2005 she made her first French, queer porn, lesbian and transgender feature film, *One Night Stand.*

In 2009 she created an evanescent group of performers for a unique European tour, with the intention of shooting her second feature film: *Too Much Pussy. Feminist Sluts in the Queer X Show,* a feminist, sex-positive documentary road-movie, released in cinemas across Europe in 2011. The film won the award for the most innovative film at the Belfort International Film Festival as well as the prize for Best Documentary in Canada and the Award for Best LGBT film at the Cannes Independent Film Festival. The entirety of her work was recognized by the Feminist Porn Awards Europe, in Berlin, in 2012. As a filmmaker, Jouvet takes part in numerous film festivals (LGBT, feminist, porn...), showing both her feature films and the many short films she directs.

Since 2012 her films have featured in the CJC's (Young Cinema Collective) catalogue. Her work is shown on cinema and TV screens (Canal +, Pink TV), and released on DVD in several countries: Solaris (FR), Fatale Media (US), Nutja Films (SW). A former member of the Queer Factory, she has co-founded different collective artist groups: TTMF, La Fem Menace, Les Productions Contraires. She is a member of Oui Oui Oui Egalité, AJL, the Association of LGBT journalists and SAFE LGBT, the Association for the fight against violence within the LGBT community. She lives and works between Paris and Berlin.

URLS:
www.TheNewParkway.com
www.FeministPornNetwork.com
MyArtGasm.com
www.emiliejouvet.com

For more information email IWantMadisonYoungUnplugged@gmail.com

SLOGANS

How do you come up with a slogan? Again we return to the vision statement and values for your filmmaking. Play around with words and what you are hoping to accomplish, and consider who your work is for. Slogans I have used in the past are "I Like it Rough, You Like to Watch"; "Tough as Nails, Sweet as Candy"; "Your Kinky Girl Next Door"; and, "Making Waves in Feminism One Orgasm at a Time."

One exercise to try in figuring out a slogan is: using index cards, write only a single word on each card that comes to mind when you think about your filmmaking process, vision and values. Try to create somewhere between twenty and fifty cards. I know for me, I get to the good stuff after I've gotten past all the words that I overuse and when I start delving deeper. Examples might be something like :

- Art
- Art House
- Obscure
- Communication
- Consent
- Desire
- Dark
- Queer
- Feminist
- Inspired
- Inspiring
- Connected
- Radical
- Authentic
- Couples
- Intimacy
- Passion
- Hard
- Hard Core
- Orgasmic
- Climactic
- Drama

Then after you have your deck of cards, start playing around with word combinations and see how they feel in relation to your vision. From the above list I might pick something like:

- We are Hard Core about Intimacy
- Inspiring Dark Desires and Radical Consent
- Creating Drama One Queer Art House Film at a Time
- Orgasmic Connection with Real Couples
- Queer Me Hard! I'm Art Core for You

You can continue to add to your deck, and you can always switch up slogans or add to them.

LOGOS

The first logo for my art gallery was an image of my Great-Grandma Goldie. The image of her, with her short hair and big cats-eye glasses, had long looked back at me from atop my mom's china cabinet in the dining room. My feminist art gallery was called Femina Potens (Latin for powerful women) and was meant to embody and encourage strength in women artists through shared stories and experiences in art, writing and performance. The image of my great-grandma conjured that history and strength that I wanted to bring to my gallery. It was also a little obscure, and people didn't always know how to say it or who it was, and this motivated people to ask questions. Our slogan was "Make Your Voice Heard."

With a friend who owned a button maker, I printed off hundreds of buttons that contained only an image of my grandmother's face. People bought them up and loved them. It was a club throughout the city. You knew someone had been to Femina Potens events if they had my grandma's face pinned onto their hoodie or messenger bag. I had friends Xerox hundreds of Femina Potens stickers, also with my grandmother's face, and the text, "Femina Potens–Make Yr Voice Heard." The stickers were radically lo-fi and gritty, and were completely cut and pasted together, but they ended up posted throughout the city.

A friend who was excellent at making stencils made a Femina Potens stencil out of a cardboard box, and my friends and I would spray stencils of the FP logo throughout SF, spreading the word and the visibility of our – at that time – small gallery. We also burned and self-screened t-shirts and patches.

I've used many of these same techniques for films, books and screenings. It's a great way to bring friends together to create materials and really take to the streets getting the word out about your film or screening. Developing a loyal local following is a great way to start with a grassroots promotional campaign.

Once you have developed a local following, you can always make your promotional materials available online for national, and even international, outreach. If you have a slogan, URL and message that are compelling, folks will feel excited and empowered as they spread the word about your film.

COLLABORATING WITH OTHERS AND LIVE EVENTS

Collaboration and live events are probably my favorite aspect of marketing a film, and a huge part of making one. What type of collaborations and live events might act as a fitting platform for your film? If your film features local bands with a following, perhaps you might put together a show featuring the bands from the film along with visuals of film footage, or a slide show of photos from the film playing. Or you can screen the trailer for the film at the beginning of the show or at intermission, and then sell the film at the show. Did your photographer capture some amazing images from the film? Maybe host a gallery exhibit of images from the film along, with a Q&A with the cast and crew about the making of the film.

Other possibilities could be workshops, panels or lectures on topics that your film tackles – remember, DIY porn is a powerful catalyst for political change and conversations. Maybe a queer dance night featuring visuals from your film and appearances from your cast is more your style. Or perhaps you could take it to a more academic level, with university lectures or presentations, or maybe the film festival circuit is more your crowd. Find what feels like an authentic extension of your film, and follow your ideas.

Discussing my film *50 Shades of Dylan Ryan* at the Feminist Porn Conference with performer Dylan Ryan and academic Sarah Stevens at the University of Toronto

PLAY WELL WITH OTHERS

Collaboration is key in the success of DIY porn filmmaking. Filmmaking involves many talents. It's inspiring, of course, but it is a lot of work, and the more you can collaborate and work as a team with friends, new and old, the more inspired you will stay, and the happier you will hopefully be at the end of your film. This way you can continue your filmmaking process for many years to come.

Think of Ways to Cross-Promote Your Film. When you're working with other filmmakers, you can work together to promote one another's films. You know how you have all these creative ideas and so much to say? Imagine if you join forces with other filmmakers, and all share resources and ideas for events, appearances, panels and online outreach.

We are stronger together. Don't fall into the mentality of "if I give away my resources or connections or ideas, maybe there won't be enough out there for me." Sharing is caring, my friends. Develop friends, build community, work together.

Put together a screening of short films or clips from films, including your own. If you have five filmmakers on the program and each is promoting the event, you will have five times the outreach. You can also promote a DVD compilation featuring similar filmmakers.

GO OUT IN THE WORLD

Get social IRL (in real life). Social media isn't the only way to let folks know about your films or get to know other filmmakers. Try going out to events in your community (and beyond) and attending events like:

- The Feminist Porn Awards
- Feminist porn conferences
- Sexuality conferences
- Erotic film festivals and art shows

IF YOU ORGANIZE IT THEY WILL CUM

Create a feminist porn event, feminist porn discussion group or dirty movie club. You are not the only one who is interested in erotic films or who wants to see DIY porn. Find folks in your area who are having open conversations about sexuality – queer or kink communities. Start to build community. Find space, even if it's in someone's living room or the rooftop of your apartment building. Part of being a DIY artist and pornographer is being able to access what resources you have, and knowing how to view those resources as assets instead of limitations.

HIRING A PRO

A lot of the time you can do it yourself, and often you will find friends, allies and volunteers who totally dig your vision and want to be a part of it and help you get started. And sometimes you might want to hire a pro.

Hiring a pro will take some trial and error, and some of that will vary depending on your budget. Maybe your vision requires a graphic design pro or someone who is ace at fundraising campaigns or creating a killer box cover. If you can't afford the pro to complete the job or just need guidance, sometimes you can hire a pro to consult with you on your vision for graphics, marketing, editing, etc.

FINDING COMMUNITY

Connecting with and finding your community is a big part of the marketing of your film. You may be asking, "Madison, how can I meet other folks that want to change the world through making pornography? Am I the only one?" Fear not, brave artist! You are not alone. You too can find other brilliant artists who want to change the world through erotic media. First, do your research and see what work is out there that resonates with you and that you are inspired by. This means you need to watch a lot of porn. As you watch films and videos, explore what about the film does or doesn't resonate with you. Which qualities do you hope to carry over into your own filmmaking process, and what do you hope to do differently? What about the makeup, the scene, the shots, the wardrobe or the narrative is conjuring an emotional response as you watch the film? Make note of your responses in your filmmaker's journal: it will come in handy as you create and produce your own films.

In much the same way that we are discerning consumers of food and clothing, and might research a company's values and ethics before making a purchase, we can apply the same research when looking for erotic films that connect with our ethics and politics. If you want to be a knowledgeable consumer of erotic films, do some basic research on the company, check out their mission or values statement, and see if it aligns with your own. Each director has a different style, and many of them started off with nothing more than a desire to put out into the world the erotic film that they wanted to see, and that represented who they were and what they desired. For your convenience, I have copiled a list of Feminist Porn Award-nominated and -winning directors and performers, along with many of my own personal favorites, as a go-to resource in your journey to find DIY porn that resonates with you.

Once you have discovered some of the directors and performers of DIY and feminist porn, start to follow them on social media and on their blogs or websites. What are the conversations that they're involved in? Join in the conversation. Tweet, message the director, send the performer an email.

The fact is that we are all very community-based, and are creating DIY porn because we desire not just to create media, but to create film that is a catalyst for conversation and social change. We want to have a conversation. We want to hear from you. We want you to join in, and to see a new generation create film that represents their own sexuality. So reach out.

Many of the directors and performers are artists, sex educators and performers, and engage in public events where you can meet them. Many of us are active at conferences around sex worker rights, feminist porn and sexual education. If you want to join in the conversation, attending such conferences is a great way to engage and to meet folks who are involved in the feminist and DIY porn movements.

Directors

- Anna Span
- Anna Brownfield
- Annie Sprinkle
- Ashley Blue
- Betty Dodson
- Buck Angel
- Bren Ryder
- Carey Gray
- Carol Queen
- Cheryl Dunye
- Creamy Coconut
- Dana Dearmond
- Dave Naz
- Deborah Sundahl
- Dylan Ryan
- Ellen Stagg

The cast, crew and extras of *The StarrLust Experience* working as a collaborative team as they shoot the entire art house erotic film in a single day.

- Emilie Jouvet
- Erika Lust
- Gala Vanting
- Ilana Rothman
- Isabel Dresler
- Jacky St. James
- Jaiya
- James Darling
- Jayme Waxman
- Jennifer Lyon Bell
- Jincey Lumpkin
- Julie Simone
- Justine Joli
- Kimberly Kane
- Lorelei Lee
- Lily Cade

- Lucie Blush
- Loree Erickson
- Maria Llopis
- Maria Beatty
- Morty Diamond
- Ms. Naughty
- Nan Kinney
- N. Maxwell Lander
- Nenna Joiner
- Nica Noelle
- Nina Hartley
- Ovidie
- Pandora Blake
- Paul Deeb
- Petra Joy
- Sadie Lune
- Shar Rednour
- Shine Louise Houston
- Siouxsie Q
- Stoya
- Susie Bright
- The Madame
- Tobi Hill-Meyer
- Tony Comstock
- Tina Horn
- Tristan Taormino
- Triangle Films
- Veronica Vera
- Wolf Hudson
- Zahra Stardust

For a more complete list of DIY porn and feminist porn directors and studios, check out www.feministpornawards.com.

Performers

- Aiden Starr
- Akira Raine
- Andre Shakti
- April Flores
- Arabelle Raphael
- Beretta James
- Billy Castro
- Dana DeArmond
- Danny Wylde
- Deviant Kade
- Drew DeVeaux
- Dylan Ryan
- Ela Darling
- Gala Vanting
- James Darling
- Jiz Lee

- Julie Simone
- Justine Joli
- Kelly Shibari
- Kimberly Kane
- Lily Cade
- Lorelei Lee
- Maggie Mayhem
- Mickey Mod
- Nina Hartley
- Pandora Blake
- Penny Barber
- Sadie Lune
- Siouxsie Q
- Sophia St. James
- Stoya
- Syd Blakovich
- Tina Horn
- Tobi Hill-Meyer
- Tyler Knight
- Wolf Hudson
- Zahra Stardust

For a more complete list of DIY porn and feminist porn performers, check out www.feministpornawards.com.

AFTERWORD

MY DEAREST READER AND DIY PORN FILMMAKER,

The time has come for us to say our goodbyes and for you to go off on your own into the world and create innovative, inspirational DIY film that shares something brave and beautiful with the world. The time has come for you to create something that you believe in, that you are passionate about.

I'm sure that you will experience wild moments of bliss and success as you manifest your visions into the world and that you will experience spectacular failures and challenges that frustrate you into dizzying proportions of overwhelming angst.

Remember we are forever students, forever learning and beyond the challenges you face there is always a solution.

Remember to take a breath, care for yourself. Artists' bodies and minds are our instruments, and self-care is a priority in the sustainability of our art and activism.

Remember you are not alone. Build your team. Collaborate and explore what resources and team players are key for manifesting your films, your visions.

Although we have come to the end of this book, know that I am here with you, cheering you on, united with you in your film-gasms and artistic explorations. I created *The DIY Porn Handbook* to empower and encourage people to pick up the camera and create the porn, create the films, create the art that they want to see in the world.

Your voice matters. Our sexual culture matters. Make your voice heard. Make your films seen. You have the power and the talent to manifest something beautiful into this world. Don't wait for someone else to do it, Do It Yourself.

With Radical Love,

MADISON YOUNG

About the Author. Madison Young is an artist, author, feminist pornographer and sexual revolutionary. Young is the founder and facilitator of the only erotic film school in the United States. She has directed 43 erotic films over the past decade, garnering numerous XBiz and AVN nominations for both her performances and directorial works, and is a six-time Feminist Porn Award winner. Her films have been screened at film festivals internationally, including the Berlin Porn Film Festival, Cinekink, and the LGBT Film Festival of Paris. Young speaks frequently on the topic of feminism and pornography at colleges, universities and conferences such as the University of California, Berkeley, Northwestern University, the University of Toronto, Yale University and Hampshire College. Young has been featured for her expertise in sex-positive culture in numerous documentaries,television and media outlets such as *Bravo,* the *Huffington Post,* the *New York Times,* and HBO. Her writings have been published in books such as T*he Ultimate Guide to Kink, Best Sex Writing 2013,* and *Coming Out Like a Porn Star.* Her memoir, *Daddy* (Rare Bird/Barnacle Books), was published in February 2014, followed by the publication of her second book, *The Ultimate Guide to Sex through Pregnancy and Motherhood* (Cleis Press). Young is currently working on a documentary, *Becoming MILF,* that explores motherhood and sexuality. She lives and works in Berkeley, California.